AF257971

PREFACE

The stories, concerning our hometown communities here in the swamps have never been told in a completely truthful way by outsiders. And it is untruthful in that most stories do not convey a true image of whom the people are deep inside and what the culture is and how the culture hasn't changed. Most stories about people in the swamp have always exaggerated the truth about our people. The actual truth in the stories about our areas has always been missed by a mile. It seems the stories are always far-fetched and carry a lie or two. That has changed with this writer and this book. Make ready for some good reading, great stories, about whom we truly are and have been for many years.

Take Pierre Part, Louisiana, for example, most of the time people always made mistakes on the name. They could not understand Part and would question a part of what. So they would flip it into Pierre park, it would sometimes become Pierre Pass, or Pierre Port, and so forth. The town was rarely ever mentioned as having any significant importance to the rest of the parish, much less to the state itself, albeit that Pierre Part contains 35% of the parish population. Yet, many surrounding areas within the State of Louisiana enjoyed our community's seafood. They indulged in our crawfish, crabs, catfish and bass that were so plentiful.

Pierre Part is the name of the founder of the community. Part is the family name. The Bayou Pierre Part flows through the section of our small town named after Pierre Part. Most people in the 1700s would say that they lived "sur le bayou Pierre Part" (on Bayou Pierre Part). Then eventually the name transferred to the entire community.

The community of Belle River was discovered by the French explorers in the 1500s and was named "La Belle Rivère". The community of Belle River, on both sides of the river, is a sister community of Pierre Part. The residents of Belle River and Pierre Part are intertwined and have intermarried among families. We do things together, we do events, luncheons, fund-raisers, etc. - Together.

The two communities sometimes operate as one when fund-raisers take place to help their local fire departments. Although Belle River now has its own fire department for many years it was called the Pierre Part and Belle River Volunteer Fire Department. The department would protect both communities, and both communities would support the fire department etc. The same thing takes place amongst many communities throughout the swamp, even those that border small towns or cities.

It is the same way throughout the majority of the swamp communities in South Louisiana. The descendants of the original Acadians, and the ones who married into those families have the same goal as the original settlers here. That goal is to make a living off the land and from the swamp in the huge swamplands of Louisiana. To raise our families in the way we were raised enjoying life in the swamp and teaching our children to enjoy life.

As long ago as the 1560s Frenchmen turned Acadians were learning from the Micmac Indians how to live off the land, how to hunt, fish, and survive. Then 200 somewhat years later their descendants were learning life-skills from the Attakapas, the Choctaw, and other Indians tribes in Louisiana. It is said, and written in books of long ago how the Attakapas taught some of the settlers how to catch crawfish in hollow tubes. A very delightful food that Cajuns, the people of the swamp, still eat and enjoy today.

In these modern times there are men such as Rodney Perera, Benjamin Landry, Mark Morgan, and Mike Campbell who are keeping the culture alive and going by teaching their children the way of life in the swamp. Teaching the culture, how things have been done, and teaching them to continue keeping on in the tradition of the swamp.

The Louisiana Cajuns living in the swamps are carrying on the true culture of Acadian ancestors from long ago.

From the very day we arrived here we began living off the land, hunting, fishing, creating new ways to farm the land, to harvest food, including animals and their pelts. We are true hunter/gatherers living life as the Acadians did when they arrived in Acadie in the 1500s

Unlike the English, les anglais, we made friends with the Native Americans. We were here before the United States became the United States, before it declared its independence. Yet, Americans call our language a foreign language. Our native language is actually more deserving than their English. The love of our culture is a part of our existence. God bless America but , also, God bless the Cajuns. We were there with Lafitte to save New Orleans. We are always there when help is needed. We are the kind that would give you the shirt off our backs but don't dare do us wrong. That is who we are; Cajun Proud.

Enjoy the stories. God Bless!

Mark Morgan and daughter Myla fishing in Grand Lake. That's what the culture is all about. Living off the land, getting our children interested and living life and loving God. Great job, Mark, Hope y'all get a wonderful season this year. Great job Myla.

Swamp Culture

Published by:
Swamp Fox Publishing
P.O.Box 376
Pierre Part, La. 70339

To order a hard copy edition of
Swamp Culture's Book 1
Second Edition
send $6.75 by check or money order
Louisiana Swamp Culture 2
P.O. Box 376
Pierre Part, La. 70339
include postage $1.25
Make checks/money orders payable to:
Morgan J. Landry

Contact editor at :
swampculture@gmail.com

Subscribe to newsletters for only $12.50 per year.
<www.laswampculture.com>

About this book:

For addtional information, address inquiries to: Swamp Fox Publishing

P.O. Box 376

Pierre Part, La. 70339

or

Email editor at swampwriter@hotmail.com

DISCLAIMER: ALL POINTS OF VIEW, EVENTS, DESCRIBED AND OPINIONS WITHIN THIS BOOK ARE THOSE OF THE AUTHOR. THIS BOOK IS BASED UPON ACTUAL EVENTS, PERSONS, AND ACTUAL HAPPENINGS. ANY SIMILARITY, IMPLICATIONS TO CHARACTERS, INCIDENTS, OR COMPANIES OR ACTUAL BACKGROUND OF ANY ACTUAL PERSON, LIVING OR DEAD, OR TO ANY ACTUAL EVENT, OR TO ANY EXISTING COMPANY, IS ENTIRELY COINCIDENTAL, AND UNINTENTIONAL. THAT IS NOT THE PURPOSE OF THIS BOOK. ALL EVENTS DESCRIBED HEREIN AND WITHIN THIS BOOK ARE TRUE AND DID IN FACT TAKE PLACE.

INDEX

This photo is by Morgan Landry and is from an interview conducted at the Miquez house. From left to right are Stephen Miquez and his wife Danell. Bonita Newsom and the famous Cajun boat-builder Edward Couvillier.

Stephen Miquez and his wife Danell were recently in a life-threatening accident when their shrimp boat flipped over , during the night while they were sleeping and the boat began taking on water. This story is being featured in the next issue of Louisiana Swamp Fox #2. Read about the horror experienced and waking up to a sinking boat.

An Accomplished musician in Belle River's swampland

-The story of Rodney Perera

Story by Morgan J. Landry

In a swamp filled with people and all manner of things in the southern part of Louisiana there exists a people who live off the land, a people who know how to survive through hard times, and a people who can endure difficulties of all sorts and still come out victorious. Anytime a person lives through an ordeal that is extremely stressful or taxing to the body that person notches a victory on the belt of life. The majority of the people of the swamp feel those victories are made with the help of our Lord and Savior Jesus Christ.

The objective of "Swamp Culture" magazine is:

1. To honor a people that have made a home in the Louisiana Swamps,

2. Capture the culture of the true swamp people, and

3. Explore the Cajun Heritage of South Louisiana through interviews and store that in the pages of this magazine.

Some of the people in these swamplands, whether they are musicians, singers, or fishermen, or all of the above, are often timid about honking their own horns and most do not want to brag on themselves. Actually pulling their teeth would probably be easier than pulling information for stories.

For the first issue of "Swamp Culture" a unique musician has been chosen.

There are numerous musicians, singers, recording artists, and talented people in the communities of Belle River and Pierre Part located here in Assumption Parish, Louisiana. There are thousands and thousands of stories and this is just one of them.

The visit to the Rodney Perera home was much beyond description, or at least beyond the capabilities of a few paragraphs.

Besides the excellent Cajun hospitality, Rodney makes the best Cajun coffee in the area running only a close second to the coffee once made by my late grandparents. I don't know that it's fair to hold him against such tough competition from that far back but Rodney does

Rodney Perera at his home studio in Belle River, La. Rodney delivers a one-man show that is simply fabulous and enjoyable to listen to and view. As a bassist Rodney focuses on runs that make the song flow . His award winning trumpet playing is absolutely beyond description and is comparable to and perhaps above that of Herb Albert's and other great trumpet players. Rodney is Cajun talent at its best.

Rodney Perera in the Atchafalaya Basin Spillway on his way to run crawfish traps. As with most Cajuns, Rodney is versatile and multi-talented.

make good coffee.

Many have been the times that visits were made to his home by invitation. Each time visiting there good, old-fashioned, home-brewed, Cajun-styled coffee was served. On top of that Rodney is a very good cook. He is also a very good host.

That is why, when this magazine was dreamed of; contemplated upon; brought to life; and then written into existence Rodney Perera was the very first person that came to mind for the first interview in the first issue of the magazine.

On my way to Rodney's place, and even while sitting in his home, as I looked at some of his musical memories and admired his two cats, I was reminded of my years in elementary school. Rodney was about two grades ahead of me, and in high school at the time. I was in 8th grade at Pierre Part Elementary School and had won 1st place in my category at the local Science Fair. My entry had been in Entomology. So I was off to Nicholls State University to compete at the state level. I remember seeing Rodney Perera there, but in a different sector of the building. He performed on the veranda of the building to a crowd on the outside. I watched him play his song and I happened to be on break later and I watched as they gave out the rewards. I asked him about that by email.

Rodney told me, during my visit that: " I did play at Nicholls in a quartet as well as with the whole concert band. I think it was called solo and ensemble day. They did give out awards and I think we scored superior but I am not sure of that because we did do that for two are three years. Long time ago...," he stated just before I began the interview.

He invited me in while he made the old-fashioned brew. Rodney uses what the old timers call "une grègue à café" to brew the satisfying mixture; and in bringing that unique Cajun flavor to his coffee.

I am not trying to give you the feeling that this is a coffee commercial and can't because of the simple fact that the mixture is not for sale. It is a home-made mixture of coffee with a Cajun flair.

The finished product is normally only available on a friendly visit to a local Cajun. Then, one will not find a large number of the locals that still brew such beverages the very old-fashioned way..

The bulk of the local people are hooked on modern ways of doing things and very few have kept the ancient ways of their ancestors. But, there are large numbers that have the old stuff stashed away. They are normally put to use during a storm when power

A newspaper clipping from the "Shopper's Weekly", depicts the winners of a third edition of "Battle of the Bands". Portrayed is the group "Nue Sounds" , the winners of a $100 prize and a recording contract. Members of the "Nue Sounds" are from left to right: Daniel Guillot; Mark Crochet; James Crochet (in front of Mark); Rodney Perera next to Mark, standing; Nelson Blanchard (in front of Rodney) ; and Eddie Dugas , far right, the group's manager.

Rodney in the group the "Nue Sound " band shortly after the recording contract. The photo was taken in front of Logi and Audrey Guillot's home and published in "Shopper's Weekly" in the mid to late 1960s. From left to right are: Mark Crochet, Rodney Perera, James Crochet, Daniel Guillot and Nelson Blanchard.

Rodney Perera -- is a Belle River native; rambling musician; bassist; guitarist; one-man band when necessary; nurse; lover of nature; lover of God's word; worked in Real Estate, loves animals including water fowl and much more.

"Once, when I was down in the dumps about music", Rodney told me that getting dropped from a band was the best thing that ever happened to him. He said that the best thing I could do was to get up, fix what was wrong and work on getting better. He informed me that, "With a lot of hard work I made myself self sufficient. In other words, I don't need anybody else to go do a gig. I can do it by myself if I have to.

He added, in saying how he lost the blues that, "The ones who did this to me could play music but that was it. I went on to run a very successful business. Got my real estate license, became a nurse, a good nurse with four commendations in first year, got into photography and also learned how to frame my pictures with frames that I made and also, became just as successful if not more, then any other local person around, playing music. Rodney won the John Philip Sousa music award when he graduated high school. "My band Sauce Piquante became one of the most successful bands around the Baton Rouge, and south Louisiana area. Our band even made Billboard magazine,"... he stated. Now, that's successful and achieving goals through hard work. Did I mention he knows how to crawfish?

outages occur.

However that might be, tasting that coffee gave my taste buds a rush to the past. Modern coffee makers can not touch this. Enter M.C. Hammer with his "Can't touch this" song. The unique flavor is only captured when using an old fashioned drip coffee pot called "une grège a café".

The taste sent my memory skyrocketing back to that time long ago when I'd enjoy sipping coffee while sitting on my grandparents porch and listening to my Grandpa's stories of yesteryear. The point? Cajun Culture is still alive. Our Swamp Culture is still kicking and might not be in danger of disappearing.

Back in the days of the last century a person would sip coffee out of a demi-tasse. That half-cup was all that was needed back then. The coffee was so strong that it lasted a while. Some of the old-timers used to drink coffee very often during the day. It seemed that it had an addicting affect. The coffee was that strong. The wallop from that small cup carried the energy and flavor of several modern day cups of coffee. Rodney's coffee is definitely authentic and as Cajun as it gets.

Being able to visit with a fellow Cajun who shares an interest in music and hasn't lost touch with his heritage and culture is a superb experience. The time spent there with Rodney Perera became a "blast".

Visiting with a friend, catching up on what's been happening while conducting an interview with a truly accomplished musician is indeed totally priceless.

The end result is an in-depth, multi layered view of how a Cajun can leave the swampland, mingle with all sort of big name stars, play music alongside "Music's" best and still not lose the uniqueness that makes that person Cajun.

The best part is, and remains that way, that Rodney still wears the same hat size, meaning his head hasn't swelled. To be able to retain one's unique culture and not allow other cultures to intrude is a challenge to anyone.

Rodney's home, which he has for sale by the way, is a beautiful two-story home that gives a grand view of the beautiful Belle River surroundings. It makes a person not want to leave the comfort felt within that homestead. That is my opinion but I feel that it could possibly be shared by others.

Rodney Perera lives with two companions. The first is a female Manx cat named Jolene. The other companion is a diversified tom cat named Norman Gene. He keeps a unique rock & roller personality about himself. Rodney says that "there's never a dull moment".

As the conversation made its way into the his musical past Jolene found a comfortable spot on the porch swing where I was sitting and went into deep cat nap mode. She never noticed when I got up from the swing to view the "Urban

Rodney with Sauce Piquante band opening for David Allan Coe

Cowboy Jam" advertising poster that Rodney wanted to show me.

The bearded Belle River musician began to describe the times spent with "Sauce Piquante" . That's the band he helped form a few years after the "Nue Sounds" broke up in the late 1960s or early 70s . The formation of "Sauce Piquante" flowed into full band mode approximately a decade after the break up of Nue Sounds.

In case you're too young to remember "Old Pierre Part" (re: the Pierre Part of the 1960s) and the "Country Club" and "Blanchard's Bar" there are photos further into the story that might supplement your experience.

One has to be sixtyish or mid to late fifty-ish or so to have experienced the "Nue Sounds" and the great bands that Pierre Part enjoyed listening to at one time in its not so distant past. Swamp Culture will attempt to bring its readers up to date with the remaining members of the "Nue Sounds" band inside future articles.

A brief run through on the local history of the area reveals that Belle River is the name carried by both the river and the town.

The river was named by French explorers and the French version is la Belle Riviére, which translates to Beautiful River.

It is common in the South for a community to take the name of the river or bayou upon where it is founded.

The people of Belle River have a way of life that dates back to the mid to late 1700s. The Acadians, typically called Cajuns in today's world, moved to South Louisiana after vacating Acadia which is now called Nova Scotia.

The locals are totally versed in English now, where once only French was spoken.

A large portion of the people still fish, some commercially, and many can still hunt and live off the land if the need arises.

It's the way of life they were taught and what continues to be taught to most of the children. One never knows when that backup system of living might actually be needed. It has been very useful to many people during times of hardships.

Belle River and its sister community of Pierre Part are situated nearly in the middle of the largest swamp in North America which is the last great wilderness known as the Atchafalaya Basin. Most of the locals just call it the spillway.

Rodney Perera is a Belle River native. He attended Pierre Part Elementary in Pierre Part, La., and Assumption High School in Napoleonville, La..

As a bassist, as a guitarist and as a musician Rodney is

Pictured here at Alex Broussard Ranch in Lafayette opening for Jerrry Lee Lewis. From left to right on front row are : George Slim Heard; Jerry Lee Lewis, Pianist extraordinaire; Rodney Perera on bass; and Mike Loudermilk, lead guitarist back row.

First reunion of the "Nue Sounds". The band has left an empty space in front of the microphone for deceased member of the band James Crochet. From left to right are Rodney Perera, Daniel Guillot, Mark Crochet, Nelson Blanchard and Ricky Guillot.

Sauce Piaquante Band: from left to right are : Mike Loudermilk; Joe Miceli , Cathy Lynn Moore , Billy Tam , and Rodney Perera.

unique in his methods of playing music.   He gets the job done. He is not one for trying to change a song, adding chords that don't belong or runs that don't belong, or over exemplifying notes on the fretboard unless such is what the situation calls for. As he has often said, "A bass in not a lead instrument".

He is very successful in the music business and a well recognized trumpet player. He is equally as good on the bass guitar. In fact, on the bass he is an accomplished musician.

A friend of Rodney, a former band mate, by the name of Nelson Blanchard was contacted for a background interview on Rodney.

Nelson is also very well known in the music industry and he will be the focus of a future article.

Nelson said that, "As a musician, Rodney can play anything he puts his mind to". My memories of working with Rodney are all good memories.

"Incidentally, he is also an accomplished bass player now. A few years ago, we had a reunion and Rodney sounded better than ever. I am hoping we can do that again soon".

Rodney plays the rhythm guitar well. He plays lead guitar, French Horn, E-flat Horn, and Flugelhorn . He is totalistic as a one-man band; he is well known for his dynamite duo presentations, when it comes to playing nightclubs with a fellow musician; and especially when taking part in a two-man band.

Rodney has played on shows with Alabama, David Allen Coe on several occasions and the same with Asleep At the Wheel. He has opened for Mickey Gilly, Johnny Lee, and twice with Jerry Lee Lewis.

He's opened for Johnny Paycheck, Delbert McClinton, twice with Hank Williams Jr., with Lynard Skynard, American Breed, Earnest Tubb, Irma Thomas, Norman Wade, Chris Ledoux, Lone Star, Sylvia, Amie Comeaux, twice with Merle Haggard, with Jimmy C Newman, Nitty Gritty Dirt Band, Billy Joe Royal, Paul Overstreet, Wayne Toups, and even Jerry Clower. Rodney said that he's   rubbed elbows with the likes of Chet Atkins, George Hamilton the IV, Crystal Gayle, and on and on.

The Belle River Musician has longtime friends in the music field including songwriter John D. Loudermilk and his wife Susan.

They've stayed in touch through the years . Rodney has on quite a few occasions loaded up his truck with Belle River crawfish, a crawfish boiler and a boiling pot and taken off for Tennessee where he's conducted South Louisiana crawfish boils in Nashville.

Rodney Perera and John D's son Mike Loudermilk started the "Sauce Piquante" band.

I Imagine

By Morgan J. Landry © 2018

I imagine, at times
that the world is better than it is;
that killing has ceased and love,
Love has taken the place of hate

I imagine, in my mind
the world turning kind,
people knowing the true God
and hatred has being thrown away.

I imagine enemies
turning into friends
that the world is nearing its end
joy is everywhere, you are my friend

I imagine death
being thrown away
life is aglow everywhere
forever to stay

I imagine rejoicing
people meeting in the sky
no more goodbyes
hugging long gone loved ones hello

Love is in the air, hate has disappeared
life is abundant fear is nowhere near
everyone talking 'bout Jesus
it's tough to hold back the tears

It's what I've dreamed about for years
the day has come, finally it has come
I can hear the great trumpets sounding
bands of angels coming

A figure on a great white horse
can it truly be
is it Jesus I see
Blessed is the son of God
Hallelujah
Alleluia!

Sauce Piquante earned top listings across the Nation and opened for top acts in the Country Music field such as David Allan Coe and Asleep At The Wheel.

The Sauce Piquante band became regular entertainment at the Kingfish in Baton Rouge. The Kingfish is still remembered as the top Baton Rouge hot spot .

The band received equal billing with Alabama, Mickey Gilley, Johnny Paycheck, and many others, in the 1980 Urban Cowboy Jam .

Rodney, when asked to describe satisfaction with his life and contentment with his achievements simply said, "It's been fun". At one point in the interview he said, "It's been a blast".

Rodney says that there are times that playing music for a living can become a job, instead of being fun, especially when it becomes a six and seven nights a week continuous gig.

However, he emphasized during the interview that the greater portion of his life has been spent in doing what he loves -- playing music. It is the music that has paid for his education in the nursing field that he worked in for nearly a decade.

His music career had small-town beginnings and during the early part of his life the thought of a career in the music business never touched his mind. He was doing what he loved to do and he was content with the moment and the current level of achievement.

His music career began   with a Christmas gift from his mom and dad.

"They bought me a Cardboard Stella," he said adding that the guitar came from Sears & Roebuck Catalog. Rodney also added that   one of the first ones to teach him some boogie woogie runs on the guitar was William "Bill" Leonard of Belle River.

He worked at the sawmill (Gaudet Lumber Company) and he'd come to the store everyday for lunch. He'd take time and teach me a few licks here and there," Rodney said.

He also said that Agney Perera, Errol Perera's Dad , taught him how to tune the guitar and showed him a few runs and how to strum the instrument.

From that point forward Rodney was hooked on music.

Throughout Elementary School Rodney focused on the trumpet. His skills improved and his goals began to grow.

By the time High School rolled around he had already joined the "Nue Sounds". The band was playing gigs at local Church Socials.

Somewhere in time, either before the recording contract or after, or even because of the recording contract, there was a name change and the group became known as the Hometown Exchange. By this time Rodney's horizons had broadened and his goals expanded enormously.

Nelson Blanchard, one of the band members of that time period was interviewed and asked about those early days with Rodney Perera. He said that, "The band members were comprised of Rodney, Daniel Guillot, Mark Crochet, James Crochet and me.

We were very close and enjoyed some great highlights in our few years together. I loved playing at Blanchard's, my father's club, with the band. I would say, it was like our home base. We practiced there and played there more than at any other place".

Asked about some of the highlights from

Rodney Perera with a male wood duck he raised and then donated to a zoo. He also raised a female. He donated the pair to the Zoo of Acadian in Lafayette.
Always preach the Gospel and when necessary use words...

those very early years Nelson said that, "Another highlight was the battle of the bands held at the Morgan City municipal auditorium. We took first place on our first night, but lost to Debbie and the Lads for the final night. We won a contract with Sam Montel of Montel Records (label of many successful Louisiana artists). However we didn't take advantage of it, having heard some bad rumors about Montel (and we were also naive about the business at the time).

We also opened up for the American Breed ("Bend Me Shape Me") at the same venue. That was an exciting night. Also, we were fortunate to perform for some functions at Assumption High School. That was great also.

"Rodney and I will al-ways share those wonderful days", Nelson said then continued with, " We have shared a camaraderie all these years that is strongly rooted in a phase of our lives that had deep meaning. We worked hard together and we reaped rewards together that really helped shape who we are.

We have stayed in close touch through the years and continue to do so", Nelson stated.

He added that Rodney is a very dependable musician. There is a very important reason the question was asked.

Dependability is one of the greatest assets of any musician. That is one of the first things an interested band will ask about a musician is how dependable is the guy. Nelson answered that real quick like with, "I can't say that Rodney ever let me down at any time on or off the stage.

Nelson also said that, "I remember Rodney almost always bringing food (many times from Buddy's) to practice. He loved his fries!

These are also the days that Rodney, like all of us, dreamed dreams of making it "big" in music.

Nelson Blanchard, in describing those early days with Rodney said that, " I'm glad to comment on Rodney. Rodney and I started playing music together after I left the Richard Brothers in the mid sixties.

Rodney was an integral part of the band, playing guitar and trumpet. Rodney was a trumpet player in school. Rodney always took his music seriously. He was into rehearsing and always worked hard to learn his parts.

The band played at "socials" in the church hall on Friday nights. We were a tightly-knit group and were learning our craft in those early days.

We loved it. Rodney is older than I am, and I looked up to him . He had a professional way about him".

By the end of high school the "Nue Sounds" disbanded and the music slowed down for Rodney . However, about eight years later he met Mike Loudermilk and Sauce Piquante was born .

At the end of the interview Rodney fired up his Yamaha rig, plugged in his bass and put his trumpet near by on a special stand.

As a one-man band he is very entertaining. In fact, if you were in another room and listened in you would guess that you're listening to a full band. That's how good this guy has become.

Rodney keeps a bass track running on his back-up machine. It runs at just a slightly lower volume than his bass. The beautiful thing about the whole thing is that his bass playing blends in perfectly with that of the machine and he's got it programed that way on purpose.

That special technique allows him to take the trumpet parts in a song and no one is any wiser that he ever quit playing bass to play trumpet.

A musician can always detect experience from the very start. The minute a song kicks off all members of the band join in and one can readily tell if a musician has experience by the way the person joins in the song. It's all part of the timing and style.

With Rodney, there's no question about it, the experience shines from the get-go. His motions are fluid and flow with the song and watching him in action is like watching a master in action. He has each part of the song mapped out and knows the most minute details and performs each with precision.

Anyone familiar with

une grègue à café is the type of old-fashioned drip -type of coffee maker that Cajuns used for years, and still used by many in the Southern regions of Louisiana.

playing a one-man band, aka solo, knows how busy a task such an endeavor can be. It takes planning, it takes attention to detail, it takes knowing the song forward, backwards and sideways and there's no question that Rodney knows the material and plays it with the expertise than only a true master can put forth., He is accomplished. He has to be, otherwise he would be a failure. Not too many one man bands are successful.

What difference does it make on how good a musician becomes. The difference shows in the bookings and how often the musician gets booked. The good ones are always booked solid, more work, better work, more money.

The Cajuns in Belle River and its sister town of Pierre Part have produced some awesome talent and this is just one of the products.

Cajuns in the Swamp doing what they love to do--.work, sing, and play music.

Then, on top of it all are the furry companions. The little four-legged critters that fill lonely spots in our lives with love and understanding wher no one else seems to understand. Sadly both of these great companions are now gone from Rodney's life but were there in full support of Rodney when the interview took place. And various visits have revealed that they were always there by his side. Below are pictures of Norman Gene and Jolene. The male is Norman Gene. The female is Jolene and is a registered purebred.

Rodney said, " She is a purebred Manx registered with Cat Fanciers' Association (CFA). The Manx is noted for hunting." Norman Gene was more of the "quiet, companion, type cat. He did not care too much about hunting sometimes. He was more interested in getting attention. Which is the reason why cats make good companions to some people.

However, he had been getting old and he was the first to go. He was a great companion and a beloved friend. Rodney said that Norman Gene is sorely missed.

And long since that interview Jolene has gone from this life and is probably busy hunting in another world where cats go.

Jolene had moved with Rodney to his new home in Labadieville, La.

He had gone through the trouble of fixing a room especially for his two companions and they did enjoy the room. Rodney continues to do gigs.

He is staying busy with bookings throughout the year. Last I spoke with home he was very busy and booked nearly every weekend of the year and almost every holiday.

He does enjoy playing music. It has become his life and he is loving it.

He is sometimes a one-man band, which he handles very well. He keeps getting calls to go back and he does go back and they love his music. What better way to live life than to live it doing what you love.

The people of the great swamp
story by Morgan J. Landry © 2017

Living within reach of the Louisiana swamplands gives many parents a perfect right to bring up their children in the tradition of the Louisiana swamps -- living off the land, being able to make a living no matter what, being able to put food on the table, and being able to enjoy real good food and the good life.

Teaching a child a love for the great swamp, the last great wilderness not only keeps a child off the street and out of trouble, but it does provide a great insight into real, Cajun -style living.

Benjamin Landry, more commonly known as Ben, wants his children to have an excellent education. He pushes his children in the right direction, helping them with their homework and pushing them to excel, to do their absolute very best for the simple reason that having a good education is very important and one of life's necessities.

However, knowing how Louisiana weather and the economy can cause hardships on a person; also knowing how many people in Louisiana are knowledgeable in several occupations he knows that it is always wise to have multiple skills and be able to work in several occupations in order to avoid hardships in Louisiana.

There are many other reasons, however. Ben said that he enjoys living the lifestyle that his ancestors showed him when he was much younger.

"I remember going crawfishing with my grandfather," Ben said exemplifying the love that he acquired for crawfishing at a very early age, then adding: "I used to go fishing my dad when I was young. We'd fish crawfish and crabs, in season."

Now , he is doing the same with his two boys. Teaching them how to fish trot lines, the proper way to grab a catfish, how to fish hoop nets, how to set crawfish traps and crab traps.

Crawfishing:

As for crawfishing, there were people eating the shellfish long before the arrival of the Acadians.

In fact, the natives in the area of Assumption Parish , around Pierre Part, the natives who called themselves "the people" also known as "the Atakapas" were eating crawfish as a large part of their diet by the time the Acadians arrived.

Brayden Landry and Isaac Landry, sons of Benjamin Landry of Pierre Part, make ready to bring up a catfish. Living the swamp-life fishing in the early morning light.

It is said, and written in history, that the Attakapas would take hollow reeds, bait that with deer meat , and catch crawfish to eat.

The Acadians called themselves des cadiens. the word was a combo of the word Canadian and Acadian but in French which consisted of Canadien et Acadien which turned out as Cadien. That is the word that led to us being called Cadjuns because the English could not pronounce Cadien.

It is said that the natives here were eating crawfish long before the first arrival of the French explorers in the late 1500s. So the tradition in Louisiana is one that has been taking place for a very long time. Even though it began with the native Attakapas it is also a very long-standing Cajun tradition that has been handed down from generation to generation.

The best thing that we can ever do for ourselves, as Cajuns, is to keep our culture going. The Cajun culture is extremely important to who we are and to whom we shall be.

Keep in mind that our French language is nearly gone, and so are the native French speakers; and Standard French does not even come close to our archaic French here in Louisiana.

The people living here in the great swamp prior to World Wars I and II , along with the baby boomers, are probably the last ones who truly experienced the real Cajun way of life.

One should also remember that while in Acadie (Acadia in English) our forefathers lived among the Mi'kmaq and some even married into that culture. A few of us even have Mi'kmag mothers because of the lack of women sent over from France. Note that there is a variety of ways to spell Mi'Kmaq and some even spell it as Micmac.

Then, when we arrived in Louisiana we lived among the Attakapas. We learned how to live off the land, off the swamp from these Louisiana natives. Some
Acadians married into the Attakapas. Some members of the Hebert family were of those

Mike Campbell and his son Braylon Campbell. Braylon was 7 at the time of the photo but had turned 8 when the magazine was being put together. He is probably closer to 9 years plus right now. Mike Campbell and his son Braylon live in Arnaudville right next to Henderson by the 1-10 weir in the Atachafalaya Basin. Mike said that where he fishes they fish in packs of 4 and 6 which makes it tougher for thieves to rob cages of their prize catch. Mike also added that he is going to make sure his son gets a good education, even if Braylon wants his own boat and wants to quit school. "I'll tell him what my grandpa told me," Mike Campbell said, "you got to get a good education first. He said that he also crabs and shrimps out of Cameron Parish. Keeping the Cajun Tradition going for the next generation.

included in that distinction.

All of that added to our distinct culture; along with us adopting many Native American traditions; plus our French culture traditions and Louisiana natives traditions all create a very unique culture that is worth preserving. Our Louisiana French Language contains Attakapas Indian words such Chaoui, the word for raccoon. The French language did not have a word for raccoon, neither did the English language because the animal is strictly native to North America. The original French explorers named it a "rat lavateur" (washing rat), and carried that word back to France. We as Acadians did not know of what the French explorers did since they were not in touch with us in Acadie. We learned to call the animal "un chaoui" when we , the acadians and the French who moved here from France, entered Louisiana and lived among the Attakapas.

Benjamin Landry, Mark Morgan, and Mike Campbell are only three of the many men in the Swamp that are teaching their children about life in Louisiana' swamp culture.

Mark Morgan is now bringing his three-year old son Madden with him everyday in the swamp while he crayfishes. Madden seems to enjoy every single moment of it.

In fact, all of these children, Mayla, Madden, Issac, Brayden, and Braylon are

Brayden Landry appears very attentive as he watches his father, Benjamin Landry, unhooking a catfish from a trot line. Brayden was about three-years old at the time the photo was taken, that was about 3 years ago. Brayden's brother Isaac Landry looks on from the middle of the boat. Both boys love fishing with their dad. Ben Landry said he loves being out on the water with his boys. "I want to show them the good life and the right road to travel," he said.

enjoying the swamp life with their Cajun dads in the last great wilderness of the United States.

One advantage that these children will have in the near future is being able to make a living and being able to stay alive no matter what.

We are living in an era where times are uncertain, where no one knows what tomorrow will bring.

Unlike the people in the city who know not where their next meal will come from during the government shutdown we are experiencing, there is one thing for certain. Swamp people can survive. Did you know that a magazine./ newspaper back in the 1860s gave us the name swamp people and even made a remark calling us swamp people?

Well it did happen, and be that as it may, these boys and girls of the swamp are learning many good things from their dads -- how to make a living, how to catch food, and how to stay alive no matter what life brings your way.

Congratulate these people if you see them for they are educating their children in the ways of life in the swamp. As has been said and sung many times before -- a boy in the swamp can survive. A country swamp boy can survive.

Besides being very instructed in educational things such reading, writing, and math these young fellas are able to secure a meal for the table, and most of them, just as soon as they can run a boat by themselves and drive themselves there will most likely do it. A great way to come up in the world, taught to work hard and enjoy life while being educated in two different worlds.

Mark Morgan is currently bringing his son Madden in the swamp with him on a daily basis. Madden is a good baiter, has the bait ready to go.

Braden Landry looks on as his brother Issac Landry, foreground, puts catfish bait into a hoop net while their dad, Benjamin Landry prepares to set the net.Educating his sons in the ways of the Cajuns.

Braylon Campbell brings up a 6 ft trap in the swamps in back of Henderson by I-10. Mike Campbell teaching his son the ways and love of the Swamp.

The Mysterious Gator Queen

Liz Choate Before Swamp People

Story by Morgan J. Landry ©

Liz Choates has been hunting alligators with her husband for years. She loves doing this and is not a newcomer to this type of hunting. Liz often hunted alligator with her father from an early age.   She was born into this type of life of life of hunting, fishing, and doing what it takes to survive; and she is a survivor.

The woman labeled as the Gator Queen is Elizabeth Ann Cavalier Choate. She is from Pierre Part, Louisiana. She is the new star on the History Channel's "Swamp People". This interview with Liz, as she prefers to be called, took place before her debut on the series. Below is her story. It begins with how she and why she got the name "Gator Queen".

It was a cloudy Tuesday morning in mid-September at C. J.. Dupre's camp. The year was 1980. The whole family was at the camp in the Marsh just out of Houma, Louisiana.

It was a long way from Pierre Part which is where the family lived in their time away from the camp.

C. J. Dupre was out in the marsh running alligator lines. That was how he made a living. It was how he kept his family fed.

Ella, Donald Richard's mom, was inside the camp washing dishes and getting a Cajun-sized breakfast together.

A fog persisted on the water this bleary late summer morning. It was nearly autumn and a chill could already be felt in the air. The fog resembled steam and seemed appropriate for the early rising sun.

At the end of the long wharf ,in front of C. J.'s camp, stood a young female child. She began clapping her hands together and her voice carried throughout the swamp when she yelled, "Oh Charlie Pie" and she'd clap again and repeat the call. She tried her best to imitate her momma's way of calling her.

Far off from the wharf, perhaps 500 hundred yards or so, a large alligator slid off a bank and headed towards the caller.

Liz's momma looked out the kitchen window and took sight of the whole thing she couldn't believe her eyes. She opened her bread box and saw that only one loaf remained and immedi-ately blamed her daughter.

Liz been feeding Charlie Pie. She knew it wasn't quite loud enough for her mom to hear, but Liz would hear about it soon. Ella, Liz' mom was grow-ing tired of the surprises with missing food and bait.

Ms. Ella saw the large ga-tor head surface 70 or 80 yards from the wharf and she saw the creature swimming towards her daughter. She waited and never said a word because she could hear her daughter calling "Char-lie Pie".

Oh what was that child up to this time, she thought. Liz had been warned to stop taking bread and to stop stealing her father's bait to feed an alligator.

Ella couldn't believe her eyes. the gator had a head on it that belonged to an 8 or 10 foot gator , this thing was huge yet there he was coming like a little bitty puppy dog as her daughter called Charlie Pie and clapped her hands while doing it.

It was amazing but still she waited to see more. Finally, Ella saw what she'd been waiting for, Liz had a five-gallon bucket of bait fish that she pulled out from in front of the ice chest on the wharf. She'd kept it out of view until the final moments.

C. J. , Liz's Dad, had said that he had bait missing and now Ella could see what was hap-pening to the bait, it was going inside Charlie Pie's belly.

Ella had heard of Charlie Pie many times but she had nev-er envisioned that it would be a large gator. After all , why would anyone name a gator Charlie Pie, after a dessert of all things?

But who would ever have thought that a large gator would come when called. She had never heard of such a thing and certainly would not have imag-ined such a thing not even in her wildest dreams. Now, here it was taking place right in front of her eyes. Oh, but C.J. would hear about this. She did not want

From left to right are: Liz Choate, Gator Queen, newly added sharpshooter to Troy Landry's boat on the History Channel's Swamp People; next to liz is her sister Dianne Richard and then Liz's brother Donald Richard, aka Don Rich.

C. J. Dupre, Liz's Dad, skinning an alligator. Time Frame is about 1978.

Ella Gauthreaux Dupre, Liz's mom, cleans gator meat at the camp in the marsh. Known as Miss Ella to many, called Moma Ella by her children, loved by many, and sadly missed. Don Rich has writ-ten a song about her titled Hey Mom. It tells of the empty space her passing left in his heart.

to lose her daughter to a gator.

Every time Liz would raise a fish out of the bucket the gator would open its mouth and wait for Liz to put it inside its mouth and he would close his jaws and swallow the food.

Ella could not believe what she was seeing, she was literally in shock. It wasn't long that the shock was overtaken by the worry of her daughter's safety. Yet, she was afraid to do anything, afraid to move, afraid to say one single word lest her daughter be devoured by an alligator. "Hey, 'tite fille," she thought to herself. Just wait until I get you away from that gator.

Momma Ella was upset. From what she saw out of the kitchen window that gator could have swallowed Liz whole. She had seen enough, she ran outside to the wharf screaming her daughter's name.

"Elizabeth Ann, Oh Elizabeth Ann," she screamed while running with a belt in her hide. "I'm going to tan your hide good, girl. Put down that bucket and come here", Ella screamed. She stopped about 20 feet away from Liz. She didn't want to get too close to the gator, she had seen what they could do. But she had never seen the likes of this. She also did not want to upset the alligator afraid that the thing would chase her and her daughter if it became upset. The water was still high enough that the gator could easily climb onto the wharf if it wanted to or easily slap the wharf with its tail and perhaps hit Liz with a glancing blow in the process.

Her own daughter had an alligator eating out of her hand. She was still amazed. She was all nervous and distraught over her daughter's safety. But she didn't want to whip the child in front of the gator. Any gator this smart might actually take up for Liz. Momma Ella didn't want a whipping from an alligator's tail.

"Je peut pas croire t'apres donne a manage a ce gros cocodrie. Tu connais quoi ce gros affair poudrais te faire?" Ella said in a fussing voice.

Translated that means, "I can't believe you've been feeding a gator. Do you know what that big thing could do to you," Ella asked her daughter.

"Il va pas me faire a rien," Liz told her mom. That boils down to, "He's not going to do me nothing".

That night, when C.J. returned from selling his gator hides Ella informed C.J. what her daughter had been up to. He had a look that Ella didn't like but she knew that he would do the best thing for all of them.

The next morning Liz was awakened by the loud report of her father's 22 Magnum. She ran outside. She feared the worse. Her heart was pounding and when she got to the end of the wharf she saw her father putting Charlie Pie in the boat. "T'a tuer mon Charlie Pie," she screamed. You've killed my Charlie Pie she barely managed to say in English.

"C'est pour ton bonheur," C.J. told his daughter in a quiet voice as he put the motor in reverse. "It's for your own good, girl" he threw at her in makeshift English.

"I cried for weeks," Liz Choate said as she recalled the moment from those many years ago. "The minute he found out I was feeding that gator he put a hook at the end of the wharf. The next morning he shot it," Liz said.

"It had to be done, it was too dangerous," her brother Donald stated in explaining why the seemingly cruel act had to take place. "No telling what could have happened to her," he said in concluding his explanation.

First part of the following Interview, conducted over phone:

Reporter: What made you choose such a hard and difficult life?

Liz Choate, (left) and Donald Richard, aka Don Rich, holding hot new single , Gator Queen. In the background in the photo used for the CD cover.

Liz: I didn't

Reporter: So, it chose you?

Liz: I can't say it was a hard and difficult life because that's the only life I knew. My mom and dad were out there and they taught me how to do it, you know.

Reporter: And you really enjoy doing that?

Liz: Definitely

Reporter: I know that in fishing the spillway or in fishing the marsh, that there's always someone running lines or traps. There are plenty of poachers. That doesn't get the best of you?

Liz: Oh yeah. It gets me angry with them But, you'll never stop that, people running lines, crawfish cages, it's always going to be there. There's nothing you can do about it, I mean...

Reporter: You find that it's better than a nine to five job.

Liz: Definitely, definitely. I worked the plant life (working in plants along the Mississippi River) for two years; and there's nothing like being out there in the woods or the swamp. Nothing like working for yourself.

Reporter: What's the part you enjoy the most? Do you like the gator hunting or fishing most or do you prefer something else?

Liz: Gator Hunting is number one. Out of everything it's definitely Gator Hunting. I was just talking to Colby. I'm serious we were just talking about that.

Reporter: Have you ever had any close calls?

Liz: Yes, Especially with the Gators. Me and my brother Joe were in the boat last year. The afternoon before I saw a large gator in the area. So, I put a line close to the water. The following morning me and Joe went out and I saw the gator when he went down. Well, we pulled him and I hit the skull instead of the soft spot (kill spot) and

he (gator) went ballistic. He went down, his whole tail and half of his body came out the water and he started banging against the boat. Joe flew to the back of the boat. I flew to the front of the boat. I didn't know whether to stand up or jump out.

Reporter: How did you get into Swamp People. How did they find out about you.

Liz: The producer was in Pierre Part. He was looking ... actually talking about Cypress.

And, Kermin Cavalier and Billy Rivere were at a crawfish stand and they (producer and crew) showed up there. The producer got on the subject of a lady fishing gators and crabbing, and all of the above. Then Kermin told him, "I've got a buddy of mine, she does it all". Then they (producer) said , "Yeah, well what's her name" and they gave my name and two hours later he was calling me. He wanted to talk with me, interview me and come meet me and everything else and it went from there.

Reporter; How do you like the filming part? The actual part where they film you during the day and the crew follows you around? Is it cumbersome, was it hard to get used to?

Liz: Well, it was kind of nerve-racking to me, but, I got used to the little guy, actually all of them. It kind of calmed down after a couple of days. It was pretty good after that but the first couple of days, I was stressed out. Having a camera always in my face, ... Oh Lord!

Reporter; I can imagine. You're used to rocking and rolling and moving on at your own pace and here you have to stop for the camera. It must be tough getting used to it.

Liz: It was kind of crazy for a little while but it was alright.

Interview 2 took place with

Don and sister Liz, aka Gator Queen, in one of a series of photos taken at a Cortona Mall studio for the cover of his new hit singl.e -- Gator Queen.

Teardrops in the Swamp
By Morgan J. Landry © 2018

Paddlin' along thru the large swamp
many times I have come along this way
I see that man has been here already this day
He has left debris in a dastardly array

A tear comes to my eye as I gaze at the trash
scattered pieces of plastic, bottles left to float
my net gathers refuse, much as possible as I pass
placing it in my boat with the other cache

A tear comes to my eye as I take in the debris
Lord, I think, if only people would think
if they would see what this stuff does
the destruction it creates, the harm they could see

But they never stop to think
in fact, they never stop to blink
as they toss out the garbage that sinks
into the mud, the weeds, in the swamp

Harm to the animals it causes, to all the fish
even to the birds, and eventually to people
don't litter, don't pollute
stop littering, please give a hoot

Liz and Donald (Liz's brother) at their sister Diane's home in Pierre Part, La.

Part of the interview covers the subject of the new song titled Gator Queen and a video made especially to promote the song. Liz took part in the video with Donald as he assumed his stage identity of Don Rich and together they made the video for Gator Queen.

Donald is older than his sister and took part in many marsh hunts for gators, also for crawfish, catfish, etc., long before Liz became old enough to go on hunts.

He and Liz did follow C.J. into the marsh on gator hunts on occasion.

The following segment is a question and answer interview which is possibly the only way to put forth Liz and Don's true feelings about alligator hunting and do the best interview possible. So directly below is the rest of the story:

Reporter; (To Don) You and Liz used to hang around together when she was younger.

Donald: Before she was there I was there. But, I chose the bandstand.

Liz: Yep, we all have a place.

Reporter: (To Liz) What was it like growing up around Donald?

Liz: It was wonderful growing up around my brother.

Reporter: (In French to Liz) Je connais qu'il et malicieux. I know he can be mischievous at times. I grew up around Donald also. He likes to pick.

Liz: Oh yeah, he likes to pick. He used to pis me off a lot.

Reporter: Especially if he takes after his Dad. Goland. Ils eté toups temps pleins de malice. His Dad was always mischievous.

Liz: That's what I hear.

Donald: I still hear srories about that. His legacy lives on.

Reporter; (to Liz) You were telling me that your Dad didn't want you around the gators too much.

Liz: He never wanted me to put my hands where I might get bit. He never wanted me to because he was scared. I'd stay in back of the boat, pretty much, but it wouldn't stop me.

Reporter: Ever got any live gators in the boat?

Liz: Well, actually me and Momma. We were in the boat one day and I was with my ex-husband. He shot a 7-footer one time. Then we put him in the boat. Then Momma turned around and he (gator) was on all fours. He was hissing (sound a gator makes when its angry). She was there, "Put him over, put him over".

Donald: (talking to Liz) What he wasn't shot in the right spot.

Liz: (Liz to Donald) No, he didn't hit him in the right spot. And he was coming, he was mad.

Reporter: (to Donald) you used to go gator hunting too?

Donald: All the time. It just wasn't my bag.

Reporter: You didn't like that, huh.

Donald: I liked it, but music is in my blood.

At this point Liz told the story of Charlie Pie and how her momma would react to finding all her bread gone.

Reporter: Did you feed him crawfish bait or other things?

Liz: Anything I could put my hands on. Fish, if we'd catch catfish;

Donald: I remember you throwing bread.

Liz: Oh, all momma's bread. Momma would get mad. She'd go in the camp. No more bread. You could hear her, "Elizabeth Ann done give it to Charlie Pie".

Reporter: So, that's your full name, Elizabeth Ann?

Don Rich: But only Momma could call her that.

Liz: When Momma was mad at me and I'd hear Elizabeth Ann, I knew it was coming. Right now they're showing me

Don Rich, the undisputed King of Swamp Pop, a member of the Louisiana Music Hall of Fame, has numerous CDs under his belt but he is disappointed that he has never scroed a nationwide hit.

and Troy in a commercial and I tell him, "If You call me Elizabeth Ann one more time...".

Reporter: Do y'all hunt together?

Liz: Yep, Deer most of the time..

Don: who, me an her? We hunted in two boats. I went in my boat, she went in hers and I watched her hunt.

Reporter: For what reason?

Don: Well, that was their living. I didn't want to get in the way, she was with her husband.

Liz: We've deer hunted together.

Don: Yep, we've gone on deer stands. Each our own stand.

Reporter: (to Elizabeth) You're a pretty good shot?

Liz: Oh yeah, I think so. I shoot year round. From November through March 31st I'm shooting Nutria all day long, day after day after day.

Reporter: What type rifle do you use?

Liz: 22 Magnum. For Nutria I use a 22 long rifle and I shoot a Remington 12 gauge.

Reporter: I read somewhere

that you use the same caliber rifle as Annie Oakley, is that true?

Liz: That's the History Channel putting that out there. I never did research Annie Oakley but I told them I shoot a 22 caliber.

Don: They wouldn't say it if it's not true.

Note: Research on the Internet has revealed that Annie Oakley was an American sharpshooter. She was the first American Super Star. Her most famous trick is being able to repeatedly split a playing card, edge on while being able to pump additional holes in the card before it would hit the ground.

Reporter: What age did you begin hunting?

Liz: I'd say about 12 or 13 years old I was running lines with Daddy.

Don: The one she learned from is the best. Her Daddy was the best.

Reporter: What year did you lose your Dad?

Liz: October 23, 2004. Lost Mom and Daddy six months apart from each other. Mom passed away on April 08, 2004.

Reporter: Both of your husbands were alligator hunters?

Liz: Jimmy Cavalier, he learned from my Dad. Justin, my current husband, he's an alligator hunter.

Reporter: On TV you're hunting with Troy Landry.

Liz: Yeah, I'm with Troy on the show. Justin will be in it on occasion. He'll pop in and out every now and then.

Reporter: You're mostly a shooter for Troy?

Liz: Yea, I run the lines and I shoot almost everyone of them (gators).

Reporter: How hard is that to do? The way they make it look on TV.... Is there a big difference from what is seen on TV to what happens in real life?

Liz: When I first started I'd just pick the line up. When you've got a big gator on that line you want to kill him as soon as you can and get it in the boat. These people let it fight around and I just wasn't use to that; I'm more of a serious person instead of entertaining, you know.

Reporter: So, the TV people want that fighting and all the trashing around.

Liz: Yep. They want the trashing around. But, it's totally different from what I'm used to. Here in the Marsh, it's different.

Reporter : In what way?

Liz: Well, You've got Cypress trees in the spillway and boscoyos (cypress knees) everywhere. We had conversations about this the whole time. He puts his line on these trees in the boscoyos. I don't fish like that. I fish away from stuff like that. Cause, I don't want to be hitting all that crap, putting my body in there trying to get these animals out. But in the marsh, it's all flottants (floating ground). You got to work at it to get them (gators) out of there but its not all those big trees and the boscoyos. .. Fishing in the Spillway with Troy, I don't fish like that...It's just totally different. We went round and round in the boat about that.

But, like I say, he fishes different, it's his way, you know, and I respect that.

Don: It's like the saying, "Different strokes for different folks".

Reporter: That's very true Don. (Reporter To Liz) Is he actually as good as they make him look on TV?

Liz: Yep! Troy is good at what he does! I ain't gonna lie. He was taught about that too. His momma and daddy taught him everything.

Reporter: (to Liz) You were telling me yesterday that the first couple of days were very rough because of having a camera in your face all day. Any other things that made it somewhat rough or tough to get used to?

Liz: That was a very difficult thing to get used to was the camera always being on me. When you finish filming all day you've got to sit down and do these interviews that last for a half-hour at a time, sometimes. It's a very tough day's work.

Reporter: (to Liz) , Does it slow down the hunting process?

Liz: Very much so. It slows down the hunting a lot during the day.

Reporter; When I called your phone, your husband answered and he was very protective of you and that is quite understandable. Thus far, has the stardom changed your life in the community? Do you have to be more watchful?

Liz: Not as of yet. But I'm concerned that when it (Swamp People) airs that it's going to get crazy. Some of the things I'm worried about is people coming by my house, you know. Most of the people are calm, cool and collected but there is always the few in the crowd that can get crazy.

Reporter: Well, that's one thing you never know about. There's always that one couillion.

Liz: But, they don't know me either.

Reporter: Troy was saying at the Chamber Banquet that there's people from all over the United States that pull up to his house and want to meet him and greet him, etc. With him, according to what he said, the people in the community point most of the crowd in the right direction.

Out of everything, do you have any favorite parts of doing the show.

Liz: Definitely. Laugh, we laugh, and laugh and laugh. Troy is a character. Then he starts to singing.

Reporter: He's not a Don Rich, huh.

Liz: No. Far from it, but he's a comedian. That's the biggest.. I enjoy that. There wasn't a day that went by that I didn't laugh.

Reporter: Can you kind of describe a typical day, start to finish.

Liz: Start to finish, a little bit of bickering , a lot of laughing, drinking a beer at the end of the day and heading home.

Reporter: How many hooks y'all run in a typical day.

Liz: Oh Lord, 70, 80, sometimes 100. We went to so many places, ran so many lines. To tell you the truth, I know it was a lot.

from left to right: Liz Choate, Diane Richard, Donald "Don Rich" Richard. Brother and Sisters living the Swamp life.

Coming in our next release, this man from Bayou Teche is living the life he loves but admits it's a tough life.

Reporter: You say you fish and hunt year round do you still trap, nutria or other stuff. They allow shooting of nutria now, I think. Is it better to bounty hunt? Is the skin (nutria) worth anything?

Liz: It's (nutria skins) not worth anything anymore. Two-years ago was the last time I trapped. I had traps all over the marsh. It's so much easier just to go shoot them. Cut the tails and bury the rest. I feed my gators with them. All over my lease. I put them (nutria bodies) in the boat and put them at certain spots where I think my big gators are going to come.

Reporter: How are some of the camera people? Do y'all have a producer that's on scene or a director?

Liz: He came a couple of times the producer. The camera guy, I liked him right off the bat. He's a down to earth little guy. I got to be real good friends with him.

Reporter: They're all from New York?

Liz: Most are from New York, Andre is from New York. Some are from California. But this little guy, if we were in a bind he'd put that camera down and jump right in there.

Reporter: Is alligator hunting similar to crawfishing as to where it leaves a smell on you at the end of the day?

Liz: Oh yeah, an alligator has a very distinctive smell. I can ride down the canal and smell them. I don't even have to see them. I can smell them and know they're there.

Reporter: It's similar to a cotton mouth.

Liz: No, it's stronger than a cotton mouth. You ever smelled one? You ever smelled a gator?

Morgan : Nope. I never hunted alligators, I've had close calls with them but that's it.

Liz: When you're going to smell a gator, you'll never forget the smell.

Diane: It's got a strong, strong odor.

Note: Diane, Donald and Liz 's sister, walked in during the conversation. She had been kind enough to allow Donald and Liz to use her home for the interview. Donald wanted the interview in a quiet place and the phone at his home is always ringing, always.

Reporter: (to Liz), So, exactly what is your husband so protective of? Have you been getting phone calls already?

Liz: It's starting, right now, a lot. They're coming from all directions. He's very protective and you can't blame him.

Reporter: No, I don't blame him at all. I knew there had to be a reason behind it all. Are you hoping to get anything else from being on "Swamp People"? However long it last, maybe once this is over with, are you hoping to maybe get movie contracts or something?

Liz: No!. Tell you the truth I don't like being in the limelight at all. The only thing that I wish that would happen is when we get into season three that they would film me on my own property. In my own boat. Me doing my own thing.

Reporter: You and your husband without Troy.

Don: On her own turf.

Liz: That's the only thing I really want. That way the people could see where my Daddy hunted all his life.

Reporter: So when you say its all flotants you mean there's no solid ground.

Liz: That's right. Other than the levees that are solid its all floating marsh.

Reporter; Do you speak French?

Liz: A little. I understand every word of it , though.

The Music

Reporter: What do you think about the song that Don wrote called The Gator Queen?

Liz: Oh, I love it. I love that song. He put it out to where it fits me to a "T".

Note: Don explained how the song had originally been written for Troy Landry and then wrote it to fit Liz.

Don: I couldn't get any response from him. Now when I did get a hold of him he told me, "Come to my house right now, I'm free". I did go. He wanted me to go through all kinds of procedures and sign all kinds of documents. Which I was willing to do, don't get me wrong, but on the other hand I didn't want to. They(History Channel) would have owned the song.

Reporter; And the song had nothing to do with Swamp People or the History Channel or anything like that and you wrote the song.

Don: It was just about alligators.

Liz: Don changed the words and it was all about going catch an alligator and it sounded so much better because it sounded so realistic.

Reporter: What's this thing I've been seeing with you in a boat with a guitar and Liz is in there with a gun?

Don" That's to promote the Gator Queen Cd.

Diane: That's the cover of the CD and she (Diane) hands me a copy .

Don: That's me, Liz and the dog is Duke.

Reporter: I haven't seen you (Don) with a guitar since that time y'all played Wilbert's (Lake View Inn on South-bay Road) and y'all were playing some Beatles songs.

Don: "Oh Darling" is what I was playing that time you walked in.

Reporter: Y'all had to go through the History Channel for that or no.(Gator Queen video)

Don: No. That's all mine. They (History Channel) would have wanted like 99 percent of the proceeds.

Reporter: Have you tried promoting the video and song on websites?

Don: No I haven't, but radio stations have it and it's catching on fire. And it's on iTunes and that's all over the world. Everywhere I play it now, Oh that's your sister.

Reporter: How many songs on the CD?

Don: It's a single. It was made for radio stations but the public can get it on iTunes.

Reporter: What are some of the words?

Liz: I have it on my computer. I'll play it for you.

Don: I wrote it about what an alligator hunter does. In the morning they hook up to their boat. Got alligator lines to run and it ain't no joke. You don't play around with an alligator.

Editor's Note: The new song by Don Rich has an upbeat Country Tempo and can match any song on the market for music, ingenuity, musical skills, words and singing. It's a super great song. The words are great and I especially enjoy the lyrics, "Got to catch an alligator, one that thinks he's so mean. He thinks he's king of the bayou until he meets the "Gator Queen".

Reporter: c'est joliement bon. That one ought to do something. That's a great song Don.

Don: Thanks, The song's really getting hot now on some local stations.

Reporter: Who's playing Fiddle?

Don: Curtis Cabello is on the fiddle; Bobby Foret is on lead guitar; On bass guitar Emmett Boudreaux, Sr. ; Michael Richard on drums, and me, Don Rich on Hammond B3 organ.

Reporter: Where was the film shot?

Don: The film you just saw was filmed in Baton Rouge. There were two producers there and a director, that was in the Cortana Mall. After we did the shoot, the engineer tells me, "I assume this is going to the Swamp People". I said no its not. He said, "What". He totally freaked out. I pitched it out to them hoping they would use it but I was denied. I was denied for "Tree Shaker" the one I wanted to do for Troy and I've been denied for that one. So, it kind of got me angry. You can't stop me from doing business. It's my creation and it's going out with them or without them. When it comes to swamp people I've been a Swamp Person long before them. Everybody from Pierre Part and the other areas are really swamp people.

Reporter: You can't get any more swamp than that.

Don: No, you can't get no more swamp than that.

Liz: Don, tell him about you laughing . I was laughing too.

Don: We were taking pictures for the CD cover and they said, "Take a serious one" and when they said that I couldn't stop laughing.

Reporter; I hope the song makes the top 10, nationwide.

Liz: I hope so.

Don: And now, recently, when I play casinos, especially the Hollywood Casino they want to involve my sister.

Reporter: Teach her how to play guitar.

Don: She's good at what she does. It's like all of us down here in South Louisiana. We don't just Love what we do but we also do what we love. That means that she loves hunting alligators and I'm a musician and I love music. We don't just love what we do we do what we love.

Reporter: (to Liz) You live on Pecan Island now, don't you.

Liz: Yep. I live there with my daughter Jessica Cavalier; my two step sons Destin Choate, and Daimon Choate; and of course with my husband Justin Choate.

Reporter: That's great! Wish the best to all of you, to Don, hope the song does super well; to Liz hope you get the best ratings on Swamp People, Ms. Gator Queen and to Dianne hope you do well and keep in touch always glad to have a fan of my writings.

Look for the Don Rich Story coming soon. Also, in the very near future, a story on Lester Richard and stories as told by him of the old days at Lil' Grand Bayou.

Lester is an excellent story teller and his stories of his youth while living under the roof of his mom and dad's home are every enlightening as to the life and culture of ol' time Pierre Part.

Life was difficult back then, some called it hard times, Lester said they got by in certain ways by using ingenuity.

You will be surprised at how they made money. The story reveals the family's heritage and love for music.

Also, Van Broussard is in our next issue. Read the story of Van Broussard and his accomplishments in the field of music.

Although you would possibly call him a Swamp Pop musician he labels it other wise. His music is not modeled after Swamp Pop music but rather after Rythmn and Blues.

Then you will also be surprised at his secret passion in life and how he has pursued it since his youth. Discover how he nearly died before his career ever became rooted.

Also, in our next publication you will find a rather interesting article on Chemtrails. These chemical clouds released from jets flying high are designed to cool off the earth. In reality there is much great damage being created, damage that could even affect your well-being.

Swamp Poems
Veracious Nuances in the Sphere of Time

By Morgan J. Landry © 2012

On a cool summer morning came, a regretted episode
I lay in bed, lost, in a deep, slumberous state
So vulnerable, so fragile, laying, sleeping,
totally comatose
A mélange of psychotic utterances seemingly sealed my
fate

On and on, a voice, incomprehensible,
so vastly insensible
Kept persecuting my inner-being, pestering me awake,
drowning in sleep, fighting to not hear a peep
I managed a few words, "Let Me Sleep"

Still on pillow, my head struggled to find my dream
Searching for the Cajun scene and monster machine
Wanting to go back to the slumber, the peace, the serenity
Tired body and soul strived to rejoin slumberous scene

Oh woe be unto me, I sighed in ancient melodic tone
I am so tired, so worn of body, let me sleep
My soul cries for rest, I am dead to the bone
Let me sleep, let me rest in shriveled heap

Crawfish

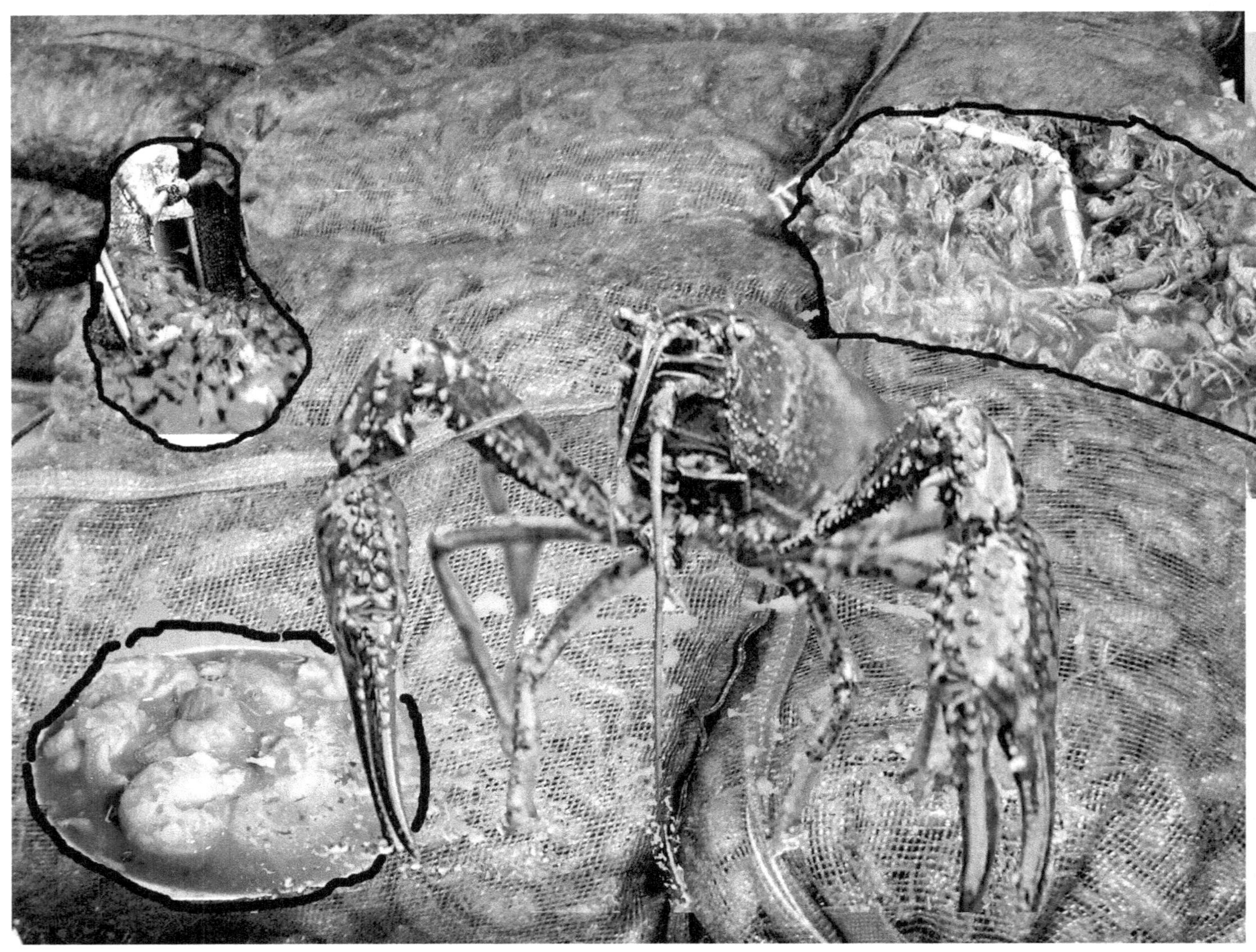

The art might not be the greatest but the intent is only to bring crawfish to mind. Promotion of any sector of the crawfish industry is not the intention of this particular article. Desctruction of the crawfish industry is also not the intent of this article either. The intent of the article as wwritten by the author is to make you think. About what? About crawfish, about the politics involved in selling our favorite delciacy and the things that might be getting shoved under the rug in the interest of the almighty dollar. There are also some stories being held back because of fear of lawsuits especially from the culprits that are to blame for some of the problems because God knows it has happened before. Certainly it is the hope that you are not too trusting and that you lookout for you and your family foremost when partaking of our state's most popular products.

by Morgan J. Landry

When traveling by boat in the spillway, known to outsiders as the Atachafalya Basin, one often wonders what harm modern technology is doing to the ecosystem.

One can see oil platforms, gas platforms, injection wells and numerous other things such as tug boats pushing barges full of chemicals, oilfield waste, oilfield products, etc.; and a few of these boats may sometimes spill minute amounts of fuel into the ecosytem as do local fisherman. With breakdowns and boats capsizing, etc. it is quite a wonder the water is still in half -way decent shape at this point in the age of man. But there are many other concerns.

Some of the other concerns are such things as fertilizers and grass killing chemicals that may wash off into the water. Example, in areas where ponds exist some chemicals might be used to control the growth of grass, etc. But there is a much broader picture than this. The Mississippi River drains over two-thirds of the United States. From North to South.

From that point up to the mouth of the Morganza Spillway there are many things that can come into play.

Farmlands drain into the Mississippi River. Countless types of fertilizers are used and some do find their way into the water.

Also used are numerous types of weed killers that find   their way into the water. Is all of this having an effect on our crawfish. Some known researchers and PhD owners say not but logically speaking it almost has to have an affect on crusteceans.

The numerous rivers and tributaries that drain into the Mississippi River bring with the flow of water an untold amount of pesticides, chemicals, and other pollutants.

Alongside of many of these rivers and other waterways are homes, farms, businesses , factories,etc. Chemicals do have a way of finding their way into the water system-- if not purposefully then otherwise.

Who checks for these chemicals? Is their any agency checking the spillway for chemicals? What agency is checking crawfish for chemicals? There are numerous questions on the minds of some people. Those questions usually pop up after someone catches cancer. These questions rarely ever have any effect on the outcome.

The answer to many of the questions above is that there is very little checking, if any. The water plant in Donaldsonville located on the edge of the Mississippi River at the inlet to Bayou Lafourche used to check for approximately 120 chemicals before the 911 attacks. The company stopped shortly afterwards due to a newspaper reporter asking questions.

The checking stopped 2 weeks after to be exact. The number of Chemicals monitored was only a microscopic part of the whole.

There are tens of thousands of different possiblities to check for and I was once told that it's impossible to check for everything. The reason? Not enough money to fund the search. Not enough money to fund the studies, the manpower etc. But the entry into Bayou Lafourche is not the entry point to the spillway. No one is checking at that point as far as it is known, currently.

The U.S. Geological Survey website, <https://waterdata. usgs.gov> provides minimal information on water quality. It provides info on amounts of oxygen in water, etc., but does not provide information on chemicals in water.

There are illusive chemicals that may slide into the mix somewhere and cause damage. That is always the possibility, as with anything.

One prime example is the Iowa Nitrogen pollution which is getting worse and worse inspite of millions and millions of dollars that have been spent to solve the problem. (desmoinesregister.com).

Nitrogen pollution is a contributor to dead zones. Called nutrient pollution it brings down oxygen levels so low that marine life can not survive. Does this not bring to mind images of crawfish trying to climb out of the traps or up the traps to get to oxygen?

Why such concerns when there aren't any reported illnesses from eating crawfish? Well, it's somewhat similar to the concerns to the deaths in the old days before they discovered cancer existed and was largely to blame for some deaths. Back then some deaths were being labeled as normal or given some other blame because of not knowing. The same with crawfish, there aren't any studies to determine or document if they retain chemicals or any other possiblities that may exist. Anyway, most believe that anything that strong would first kill the crawfish before it reaches market. Not necessarily true in all cases.

There is a publication that addresses toxcitity levels of pesticides and advises precautions when spraying near ponds.. The Southern Regional Aquaculture Center's publication No. 4600 published in October 2013 offers toxicitiy levels for differenct pesticides etc., when used near ponds. That offers concerns to prevent killing the crawfish.

Now, one LSU professor states,(further in the story) as does the publication, that anything over a tolerable level will kill the crawfish. That, is a known factor. It is also said that any amount would kill the crawfish before it enters market, and the crawfish would not make it to market. Everyone knows that for intolerable levels.

However, what about very small minute levels that crawfish might be able to tolerate. Example: Such as a little bit of gas dropped in the bottom of the boat that doesn't kill or touch the crawfish but the smell poluttes the entire sack. Anyone ever gone through such an experience?

The matter of these pollutants and their possible ties to the causes of cancer here in "Cancer Alley" is a main concern. It actually became an obession when my wife was being treated for cancer because of what I was witnessing while bringing her to treamtents .

If you're at the hospital as an observeur, not as a patient, and bring someone to receive treatment you will notice the people affected moreso than those who do not travel there or ever observe such treatements. The amount of people there are large in number. If you never go there, then there are chances that you might never know of the number of people affected.

For one it's a privacy issue and secondly most people do not advertise the fact that they've contracted cancer. It's not considered anything to brag about. It is a very depressing time in life. Most often, when a person contracts the big "C" it is a time that the person wants solitude and doesn't want a swarm of visitors because the disease has a way of converting a person to want to be alone.

In 2009 I became commissioned, by way of duty and vows as a husband, to be chief bottle washer, cook, housekeeper, and caretaker of my wife and my normal duties were doubled upon me by this thing called cancer.

In driving my wife back and forth for care at the state funded hospital in Houma, the place called Leonard Chabert Medical Center, I was a witness to many things of which were actually forced upon my vision. Forced by way of not having a choice as to whether to be there or not.

On the third floor of the hospital in Houma is the surgery clinic, the operating rooms, the recovery rooms and the cancer threatment rooms, one of which is the chemo-therapy dispersing area. The room has about 25 recliners, maybe more, equiped to hold IV units and that is where the patients sit to receive their chemo in prescribed doses. For some patients it is twice a week, some three times a week and some once a week. The dosage dispersements were also configured to where the patients would be there on Wednesday which is the day that the oncologist would be there to examine his patients.

The routine is very grueling, especially for the patients. However, it is an ordeal for the non-patient also. The task of waiting for the passage of time is a nerve racking ordeal. Listening to talk, the sharing of stories, of personal battles with cancer enlightens a person of what these people go through. The conversations relieve some of the boredom. It makes the time pass by faster. Some of the stories are heart breakers.

Many a time, while seated next to my wife in that treatment room has the presence of God been felt. The presence of angels, amidst prayers being said and of talk of God being said. But, also were the times, although not as numerous, not even close, that it seemed as though death itself walked the halls. One could sometimes sense the presence of the Angel of Death seeking a victim, or was it the devil seeking someone to devour. God only knows on that one.

One day I felt its presence and wrote of the encounter within the tale of a poem. The feeling struck me as weird and other-wordly, which was the being able to feel the actual presence of death as though it was roaming the room looking for its next victim. It was as though he was searching for someone to claim. I still don't know whether he passed me by or not. Only time tells the end results of such encounters, or such a presence.

What has all this to do with crawfish? In a way it has everything to do with crawfish, seafood and the things that enter our local environment.

During the long days of waiting at Chabert my wife and I met many people from the Pierre Part area. Some were from Belle River. A few came from around other parts of the state, but some once hailed from Pierre Part or Belle River and moved away for one reason or another.

All these people, most followed by a spouse or other close relative, were there for cancer related reasons. Some were just finding out they had cancer having just recently been diagnosed. Others were coming back for checkups

and waiting to see the doctor while others were in the middle of treatments. In one way or another most of these people, at least the majority, were there for cancer releated reasons.

The majority of the conversations held between patients and non-patients had to do with cancer, what the people had been through thus far, the pain, some of the foolishness (or what they considered foolishness) involving the government system, the hospital system, etc.

There existed a lot of joking between the nurses and the patients. There were times the conversations would turn serious, however. The environment was a very somber one, when that took place. It was only through joking that the somberness was removed.

A change in conversation would take place when a new patient would come in. There the few occassions that there would be one or two from Pierre Part or Belle River and then sometimes several a week would come in. Then the talk would turn to what is going on , why are so many people catching cancer, where is the cancer coming from, what is causing it, etc.

Soon the conversations would trun to crawfish and other types of seafood.

"Te conais pas quois qu'ill mettent dans l'eau ces jours ici", someone would almost always say. Translation: You never know what they're putting in the water these days. That is a mouth full and then some. Look at today's water sources and those delivered to our tap water with reports of Ecoli in the water. Although in minute amounts who wants to drink such things.

"C'est plus comme c'etait" would also come around at one point or another. Translation: It's no longer like it used to be. That is certainly true. Some

things are better some things are worse. That brought to mind visions of when I was young and when my father was working for the State. They would come in front of the house, down the bay, and I would see them spraying the chemicals onto the water lilies and on some of the tall grass, rushes, etc. I know now that all that poison was going into the water.

"tu connais pas quoi qu'il y a dans cette eau. Avec toutes les puits d'huille qu'il ya ces jours ici" Translation: You never know what's in the water, what with all the oil rigs in the water nowadays. That would most certainly would be heard at one point or another.

"Tu peut pas prendre cas du government. Ils vont dire n'importe de quois pour tu taire" came up quite a few times. Translation: You can't trust the government, they'll tell you anything to shut you up.

"Je dis pas grand chose parce que ils'ont a plein qui fait leur vie avec ça" was heard at least severals times per conversation. Translation: I don't say much because there are many that make their living with it. To me it was like who cares if someone is making their living, if it's taking lives let's do something. It's the same as with cigarettes. If the cancer sticks are causing that many deaths remove them from the market. Nope, it's all about the money, that's what it is.

The bulk of the conversations reminded me of the conversations of yesteryear when I witnessed some of these same conversations at my grandfather's home which took place sometimes in the kitchen, sometimes in the living room and sometimes on the front porch.

There were always five or six people talking at once. Some of the wives were talking to other wives (at the same time

the husbands were talking), or somtimes nurses would join in, while the husbands carried on their own conversations with whomever. A few conversations carried bits and pieces of French, some were all in French while others were half French and half English and some were conducted in broken French. The miraculous thing is that everyone understood what the others were saying and no part of the conversations were missed by anyone, except perhaps the nurses. There were times that the nurses would join in on some of the more noteworthy parts of the conversation such as: "You know it could be in the seafood," one said noting that it is a common factor across the board because nearly every single person in that room eats crawfish, catfish and other types of seafood caught locally.

My favorite phrase was: "C'est oblige d'etre quel que chose" and I would agree it's definitely got to be something, there's no doubt about that. Translation: It's got to be something.

It seemed that some of the nurses understood French, same with some of the patients. A few would speak French, others would answer in English. Every now and then a nurse would join in, always in English. One said, "You know my mother talks French". One or two said they had relatives in Pierre Part.

The element of surprise here was that everyone agreed that something had to be feeding the cancer epidemics that were occuring. Most agreed that it was foolish to blame everything on cigareettes. "C'est la premier chose qu'ills disent" (It's the first thing they say) one person said and agreed that cigarettes could not be the blame for every single case of cancer. "J'ai jamais fumé presque toute ma vie" another person said. Translation: "I have never smoked in my life, or all my life I have never smoked." remarking, also adding that the cancer wasn't in the lungs.

Just about every single person took the time to say, "C'est temps qu'ills faisent quelque chose". Yep, it's about time they do something, whoever it needs to be, something must be done. Too many questions have remained unanswered for too long. How long?

I can remember talk of similar things as far back as the time I was eight-years of age when I'd go set-netting for crawfish with my grandfather.

Although the man has been deceased since 1987 I can still remember what he used to say when I wanted to go set netting for crawfish around 1959 and 1960.

"Tu peut pas attrapé ça n'importe des où, non" he would tell me in trying to make me understand that one just doesn't go fishing just anywhere. He always made the point that one had to pick a place that was clean; and this was clean meaning clean water (not clear) away from houses where sewage might exist and away from any trash piles.

Back during that time outhouses were everywhere and some people, the ones who could not afford an outhouse used chamber pots (pot d'chambre) and would throw the mess in the edge of the woods in back of their homes.

Of course, everyone kept a chamber pot in their home for those times when it was inconvient to make a trip to the outhouse.

"Je ne veux pas des écrevisses qu'a goût d'merde," my grandfather would tell me saying that he didn't want crawfish that tasted like sewage or that came out of anywhere where sewage might exist.

The only other thing

that I can remember that could have been harmful from that time frame were the many trash piles scattered everywhere. Some people had trash piles in back of their homes, some along the bayouside and I'm sure each contributed their own small portion to polution of the environment. Pierre Part Bay, the edges of South Bay and North Bay along both sides of Bayou Pierre Part all had small garbage dumps along the water's edge. Those trash piles were cleaned up in the late 1960s through the effcrts of Ray Crochet and other community members. Crochet, with the permission of the parents contracted the help of students and on certain weekends there were litter drives and the students put the trash in bags alongside of the roadways and the bags were picked up by other workers and placed in large trucks and brought to a legal dumpsite.

Even at that time, however, chemicals in the water and other harmful materials did not exist as abundantly as in today's world.

Nowadays there many reasons exist to think about problems that might exist with crawfish because of the water.

If you're skeptical and believe that the problem does not exist then go for it. All arguments are welcome. However, keep in mind that Louisiana State University has disclosed that the fat in crawfish can absorb pollutants. By reference to the fat LSU describes it as a pancreas of a type that works similar to a liver.

To put a more professional prospective on the issue or question at hand I sent a list of questions to an LSU official familar with some of the questions asked. The following questions were placed to Robert P. Romaire. He was the only person I could find through internet research at the time this article was written.

In responding Romaire replied that: Your questions deal with seafood safety and we have better experts at LSU to answer some of your specific questions. He provided the names of experts that will be contacted. Romaire took time to answer the questions but first pointed out that, "I'm going to quickly respond to some of the questions that have crossed your mind. Please recognize I am a crawfish aquaculture biologist and not a seafood safety or public health safety specialist," he said. The questions and his answers are directly below:

1.   Could there be a link between a high rate of cancer in the area and crawfish and water quality?

A. Not likely and highly improbable. From what I've read life style choices in Louisiana – smoking/obesity – are often found to be responsible for higher incidences of cancer in certain areas of Louisiana. I am not aware of any studies that have been conducted on chemical residues in edible portions of crawfish that are

public health concerns. You could contact the Department of Health and Hospitals Center or Environmental Health to see if they have additional information that I am not aware of.

2. Can an injection well in the area where crawfish are being harvested affect crawfish and the safeness of the meat.

A. Don't know. What is the well injecting? Unless crawfish are being sampled for toxins and residues, which is doubtful, there is no database.

3. I've read before that crawfish can absorb pollutants in the fat of their shell and that is advisable not to suck the heads but many people in this area do. How bad is that for a person to do, that is sucking the heads and ingesting fat.

A. It is true that toxins are most likely to accumulate in the fatty tissues/liver tissues. The "fat" in crawfish is not fat, but rather the heptopancreas which is basically a liver and pancreas in the crawfish. Toxins are most likely to accumulate in the hepatopancreas vs the tail meat. Studies have shown this. How bad is it for a person to consume crawfish fat? It would depend on what is in the fat, if anything, and how much is consumed.

4. Do you know of any studies on water quality in the basin?

A. Contact Dr. Bill Kelso, School of Renewable Natural Resources, LSU, on water quality studies in the Atchafalaya Basin. They have conducted some nutrient chemistry research in the Basin and he will mostly likely know if other governmental agencies or universities have been conducting water quality research in the Basin, either past or current studies. Dr. Kelso and his colleague are and have studied to varying degrees ecological changes in the Atchafalaya Basin and he can better address these changes than me.

5.   Is it possible that chemicals in the water, from oilfield operations in the area, could be affecting crawfish and the safety of ingesting the meat or the fat?

A. All I can say is that past residue studies that have been conducted on crawfish from the Basin and aquaculture ponds have not shown there to be any major concerns with pesticide or heavy metal accumulation in crawfish. But these studies were conducted 20 + years ago. That said, oil field drilling operations in the Basin have long preceded those studies that were conducted two decades ago.

We have encouraged that the crawfish industry, for both wild and farmed, consider supporting research that would update residue analyzes for edible components (tail meat and "fat") for crawfish in Louisiana, be either it wild caught or farmed. When persons such as you ask these questions today, all we can do is cite the residue studies that were conducted in the late 1980's and early 1990's.

Editor's Note: It's high time that people start asking for studies, making phone calls to representatives and senators and let's get some studies and find out the truth.

But it is not common for short-lived animals that feed low on the food chain, like crawfish, to bioaccumulate any significant amount of toxins that would make their consumption harmful. Any seriously toxic compound might kill the crawfish in which case they would not be available to be consumed by humans. Crawfish are highly sensitive to certain type of chemicals, such as pesticides, and they are more likely to die than to bioaccumulate these compounds.

If you are looking at the basin as a whole, it is not probable that oilfield operations are affecting the safety of crawfish and their ingestion. In an area immediately surrounding/adjacent to an oil field drilling operation that potentially might be different but without data to review I would not know", Romaire said.

Please note that in the next issue of Swamp Culture the same questions will be posed to the experts recommended by Romaire. I am curious as to what the other experts will say.

Chemicals are not the only threats that should attract worry. There is one threat concerning raw crawfish that has been reported in other areas. Fortunately the majority of the people in this area do not eat raw crawfish but to those who do there is a health threat being made known.

Physicians at Washington University School of Medicine in St. Louis have diagnosed a rare parasitic infection in six people who had consumed raw crayfish from streams and rivers in Missouri. The cases occurred over the past three years, but three have been diagnosed since last September; the latest in April. Before these six, only seven such cases had ever been reported in North America, where the parasite, Paragonimus kellicotti, is common in crayfish.

"The infection, called paragonimiasis, is very rare, so it's extremely unusual to see this many cases in one medical center in a relatively short period of time," says Washington University infectious diseases specialist Gary Weil, MD, professor of medicine and of molecular microbiology, who treated some of the patients. "We are almost certain there are other people out there with the infection who haven't been diagnosed. That's why we want to get the word out."

If you've boiled crawfish recently you've probably noticed white spots on some crawfish, sometimes its almost

every single craswfish that is infected. In the recent past its presence was not common for crawfish to have these spots. The spots are caused by a virus. It is called the White Spot Syndrome. According to LSU the virus does not affect humans. The disease first started in China and Thailand and then to Hawaii, then to Texas and now to Louisiana.

It should also be noted that one of America's most popular pesticides uses a chemical called glyphosate which has been proven to be a carcinogen. Americans are much too loose with the use of the pesiticde. In fact, many do not wear protective clothing or equipment and in many places it is sprayed along the edges of school grounds without proper safeguard. Is there the possiblity that this chemical could find its way into Louisiana waters. It does find its way very easily into Louisiana waters, a little too easily, in fact. There are questions to be asked and Swamp Culture is making phone calls, asking the right

questions and getting answers.

What people are not realizing is that big money is taking the place of precaution for the safety of the people. Those are people such as you and I.

Shouldn't the total safety of the product be the foremost quest in the forefront. Should not we be worried about our families and what our children and relatives are eating? The one thing in my mind is whether of not the safety of the people is being considered or is the product and the almighty dollar that is being placed ahead of safety.

The LSU professor is possibly correct, after all she has made a career of this. Sometimes a minute amount, however, as in parts per million might deliver something unwanted and it might not affect the crawfish right away. Only God knows the extent to which people will go to in order to make more money.

Boudro et Thibodo

Thibodo was sitting in a friend's home one afteroon just past Bayou Goddell when in walked a pirate. The pirate had a peg leg, a hook and even wore an eye patch. It didn't take Thibodo long to figure out that the pirate was his old friend Boudro.

It had been over 15-years since they'd seen each other and they soon caught up on old times and brought each other up todate on the latest. Finally Thibodo got the nerve to ask his old padnuh , "How did you get the peg leg? Boudro explained that he'd gotten washed over-board in rough seas and a shark bit off his leg just as he was getting pulled back onboard. Thibodo said, "ooh, that must have hurt". Then Thibodo said, "Well what about your hand"? Well we boarded a ship to raid it and someone cut it off with a sword. "Ooh that must have hurt," Thibodo said then asking, "Well what happened to your eye"? Boucro said, "Sea Gull droppings". Thibodo thought about it then said, "How can Sea Gull droppings mess up your eye". "It was the first day with my new hook, " Boudro said.

Writing Services

Includes Ghost Writing, Editing, Biographies, memoirs

contact
swampwriter@hotmail.com

Met a girl today, oh boy
By Morgan J. Landry ©2018

Met a girl today, did not know what to say, what a girl
She sent my mind awhirl, really rocked my world,.
I wished she were mine I did say; thought about her all day,
It feels right, she was so kind, Wanted her to know my heart; I prayed.

Lord, this girl troubles my heart, she gave it a jumpstart
I have never had this happen before, I thought it ancient lore
I thought it was fantasy, but now I am a casualty; of love,
I need your help Lord, I pray to you up above, grant my heart's desire.

I met her again, we became friends, I looked into her eyes, saw myself in there;
I wanted to be in here heart; stayed in mind, make her mine, I humbly prayed
Maybe in time, probably God's time, I will get to hold her tight, one day.
I thought of her eyes, her hair, the touch of her hand; I bowed by head to pray

Called her this morning. Her voice touches my heart, yes it does;
It sets my heart to burning; It sets my mind and soul abuzz.
I asked her on a date; I was so scared to, the silence before she answered
My brain did batter; nothing else mattered except hearing her say yes

---

Pierre Part in the Civil War

Approximately 156 years ago the small rural community of Pierre Part had a portion of its residents take part in the Civil War.

One of those residents is Jean Baptiste Mabile. He enlisted as a heavy artillery gunner in the confederacy. The information was obtained through the Louisiana Secretary of State website in the site's archives under conferate pension applications. Mabile is listed in First Regmiment Company B of the Louisiana Militia.

The photo on the right was obtained from Carrie Leonard Smith . Carrie and her sisters - Mary Jane, Deanna, Dorothy, Catherine Ann and brothers Charles and Bill are decendants of Jean Baptiste through their mother Therese (ToleMae) Blanchard who is the greaat, great grand daughter of Jean Baptiste and the daughter of Wilson and Alice Marie Mabile Blanchard. Alice is the great grandaugther of Jean Baptiste Mabile, according to available records.. Her father and mother are Sylvain Clebert Mabile and Melanie Comeaux Mabile.

Jean Baptiste Mabile was born in 1841, according to one genealogy record in current existence.

According to that data Jean Baptiste would have been 20 years old as he enlisted in the Confederacy. It is not known

Jean Baptiste Mabile and his wife Marie Annette Guillot. Photo provided by Carrie Leonard Smith. Jean Baptiste served in the Civil War in the heavy artillery division in the Confederacy.

Pierre Part in the Civil War cont'd

whether he enlisted voluntarily or was forced to enlist. During that time the troops enlisted when Confederate troops would march into the area. Those who did not volunteer were most often forced to enlist in the service.

Augustin Joseph Richard was born in 1887 and is the son of Auguste Richard who was born in 1845..

Augustin Joseph Richard is the great grandfather of Morgan Landry, the author of this magazine. When I was yournger, writes the author, he often told me stories of how his father and grandfather (Theodule Richard, born 1817,) had told him of how it was during the Civil War.

My grandfather, Claiborne F. Landry often told me similar stories of how it was and both men told me nearly exact stories of what had taken place during the Civil War in Pierre Part. Both of my grandfathers told me on numerous occassions that most of the men had hiding places in the woods, some even had pits dug in the ground to use as hiding places from the soldiers.

I was told that it did not matter which side it was that if an able bodied man was captured he was taken in and inducted into military service.

Those who tried to run away would get shot. There were some that volunteered but quite a few did not want to serve because they did not see a reason to be involved in such a foolish skirmish. The majority had nothing to do with slaes and did not want slaves and could not afford slaves even if they would have wanted slaves.

Jean Baptiste Mabile has the following records in the National Archives -- Mabile, J. B., Pvt. Co. B, 1st La. Hvy. Arty. (Regulars). En. Oct. 20, 1862, Assumption Par., La. Present on all Rolls to April, 1863. Rolls June, 1863, to Oct., 1864, Absent, refused

parole, sent North, Roll March and April, 1865, Prisoner of War, sent North, July 11, 1863,

dropped order Hdqrs. La. Arty. April 30, 1865. Federal Rolls of Prisoners of War, Captured

Vicksburg, Miss., July 4, 1863, refused to sign parole, sent to Memphis, Tenn., July 18, 1863,

transf. to Gratiot Str. Military Prison, St. Louis, Mo., July 26, 1863. Forwd. to Camp Morton, Ind., Aug. 2, 1863, released on Oath of Allegiance, Jan. 3, 1865. Note: Captured at Vicksburg,

Augustin Joseph Richard
1887 -1970

Miss., July 4, 1863, refused to be paroled and asked to take the Oath of Allegiance to the United States and be released.

One example of those forced into service is :

Landry, E., Jr., Pvt. 1st Co. Chasseurs a pied La. Mil. On Roll not dated, ordered into the

service of the State of Louisiana. En. Feb. 24, 1862.

ATTENTION READER: If you have any stories of the Civil War in Pierre Part, Louisiana or in Belle River, Louisiana or any other location in the Bayou State you are welcomed to submit photos and stories for placement in Louisiana Swamp Culture Magazine.

Stories from Thibodaux, Houma, Napoleonville, Morgan City, Paincourtville, Plaquemine, and other areas are welcomed.

The Pirate Jean Lafitte in the Swamp

by Morgan J. Landry ©2018

This is a true story, just as all stories printed in Louisiana Swamp Culture Magazine are true. It is based on research, and based on fact.

There have been tall tales published about Jean Lafitte, the famous pirate, but such stories have never been printed in

the pages of this magazine.

Jean Lafitte was born in St. Maloes, France. It has been said that he grew up in Saint Domingue. He was raised by his uncle. Lafitte had a profound hatred for the Spanish and always targeted their boats, to rob, because of the way they treated his father.

His last name is really spelled as Laffitte but "Les Anglais" always spelled it as Lafitte. He considered himsself a privateer and did not like being called a pirate in much the same way a thief does not like being called a thief.

One thing that must be told is that inspite of or irregardless of his choice of livlihood, Laffitte is and always will be a hero, even if the State of Louisiana did not want to declare it as such.

General Andrew Jackson arrived very short of ammunition, before the War of 1812 (aka the Battle of New Orleans). He also arrived short of supplies and short of guns due to a skirmish with Indians. Even if he had not arrived short of ammunition he would still have been short of the ammunition needed for the Battle of New Orleans. None of his

men were familar with the swamp and it is very doubtful that any of them had any idea as to how to fight the British. It is Laffitte who warned the State of Louisiana and General Jackson of the impeding danger from the British. It is Laffitte and his men who are responsible for saving New Orleans, no matter what Louisiana said.

I also do believe that it should be duly noted, because of extensive research recently completed, that the majority of the people who put him down, during that time, were probably more crooked than he was and more deserving of jail time than Laffitte was, at that time.

However, down to more localized history regarding Jean Laffitte and his brother Pierre Laffitte.

It is a well-documented fact that Jean Lafitte spent much time in the courts of New Orleans trying to retrieve his property stolen from him by local government of the time. He also spent much time requesting compensation for his losses of gunpowder, cannon shells, bullets, etc., that he provided not only to his own troops, but also to General Andrew Jackson's men and to any others who came to defend New Orleans.

Research depicts that if it had not been for the extensive supplies of Jean Laffitte that the war of 1812 would have had different results. Laffitte even wrote to the President of the United States and, still, not a word of recompensing him for his expenses in the war of 1812.

It is at that point that Laffitte returned to his old ways of pirating, looting Spanish war ships, cargo ships, etc.; looting British war ships, and cargo ships. Laffitte had a Letter of Marque from France authorizing him to loot Spanish cargo ships on the high seas. In French that is "une lettre de marque". A letter of marque is a license to fit out an armed vessel and use it in the capture of enemy merchant shipping and to commit acts that would otherwise have been constituted as piracy. Thus the reason why Laffitte called himself a Privateer.

It is said that these semi-official entrepreneurs, carrying government-signed letters of marque and reprisal, and known as privateers, also were a significant force in commerce raiding up until the nineteenth century.

That did not phase the United States Government, and did not make a bit of difference. Government patrols began making chase on Laffitte and he had to go into hiding many a time. And, many are the times that Laffitte sought refuge in the swamps.

Money has always been at the root of greed and Louisiana

has its share of the greed.

Greed causes a wanting for more and Jean Laffitte was always wanting more and always greedy, always in search of new treasure to keep his lifestyle going. But, beginning aournd 1824 that began to wane greatly.

Government agents would chase him, when they would get too close, at times, he would just throw the treasure overboard never taking note of the spot.

There were times he would stop and bury the treasure, other times he would sink the entire boat.

There is believed to be one such occassion that took place just outside of Belle River, Louisiana, a community about 8 miles outside of Pierre Part.

About 4 miles somewhat west of Belle River, towards Bayou Pigeon thre is such a boat. The mast of the boat sticks out of the water during times when the water is low.

There are notations within historical documents that denote Laffitte as having had places of refuge in the Thibodaux area, the Napoleonville area, the Labadieville area where relatives lived, and even the Donaldsonville area. But it wasn't until years after his death, around 1878, that a discovery was made inside the pages of an ancient journal, written in French, the story tells of the property of the widow of Jean Lafitte being sold to resolve a succession. The exact location and the details are stored in the clerk of court's office in Napoleonville.

In a bayou like this one, about 30 feet in a cove lies the boat of Jean Laffitte. Only the mast is sticking out of the water, and that is in times of low water levels.

An advertisement ran in the pages of The Assumption Pioneer in the 1870s announcing the succession of the property of the Widow of Jean Lafitte. No, that is not a misspelling. That is how the name was listed.

Stories are told of the property being dug up by would be treasure seekers. Notations have been discovered that state that not a stone was left unturned in that incredible search for Jean Lafite's treasure that was never found. If it were true that Jean Laffitte's ghost roams the area they would all have been shot by ghost bullets or had their heads removed by a ghost.

In the area of Pierre Part there were always rumors of treasures of Jean Laffitte buried in the woods. The author lived in an area that was very close to Lake Verret. There were always boys bragging about how their grandfather told them of a treasure buried by Jean Laffitte by such and such an oak tree. We would all take off on an adventure in search of a tree with the mark of JL on the tree. Those were such exciting times.

My grandfather happened to be the family storyteller. Some of the stories he told really sparked my imagination. He had always been the family story teller for as long as I could remember. Many people said that most of his tales were true. I enjoyed believing that; and I still do for one of his stories scored a life-time memory for me. Even now, I still remember many of his porch-told-yarns.

He was disabled. He had been crippled during a logging accident while working deep in the swamp. The long boring days of summer seemed to move him to telling stories. Having company that would listen is what moved him to telling stories more than anything. He and I would spend many an evening keeping my mind enchanted with lumberjack adventures turned tales.

Those many varied testimonies of his would send my boyhood mind traveling down the lonesome cypress-tree-lined bayous near Lake Verret. There were many days that I spent searching the old logging trails near my home for glints of silver fallen from a pirate's chest or from a boat bumping into fallen logs. I would dig holes at the bases of trees where people had rumored treasure might be buried. I was a born treasurer hunter back then. My grandfather's stories kept my mind wandering in anticiapation of finding treasure.

There were tales he told that often kept me intrigued with visions of Jean Lafitte. I always thought of treasure, especially when he mentioned a sunken boat. I imagined finding some of that buried loot. One tale that he told was of a sunken boat buried in silt down a narrow bayou. He told me that if a person looked at the right place at the right time that the end of the mast would be there barely sticking out of the water. He added this was just during times of drought that the mast could be seen. The story he contended to be true. It had my mind burning with desire to be off in search of the treasure of Jean Lafitte.

I can still remember questioning my grandfather about the chest and asking him if he could bring me to see the location where the boat was sunk. I would do this until his anger would explode like the long-barreled shotgun that he used in hunting Grosbec. That bird named a Grosbec is a Cajun French name for a blue heron that Cajuns love to eat. It is against the law to kill these birds and always has been. But, Cajuns still kill them and eat them at the camp. It's a mighty expensive meal if caught.

After several weeks of prodding him my grandfather gave in and agreed to bring me to the area where he said the boat had sunk. He bid me promise to never tell the exact location. I promised that I would not as long as he was living.

The trip to Bay Natchez would be a long one, especially with my grandfather's boat. A 7.5 Evinrude on a 12 ft. cypress bateau does not travel very fast.

But it was the place where the sunken boat lay beneath the water. That is where I wanted to go.

I just had to catch a glimpse of the boat mast. I wanted to see it for myself. Then finally, one day in July of 1966, we were on our way. We were just outside of Bay Natchez in the area of Old River, close to where this waterway joins Belle River when he stopped the boat.

He pointed to a small cove. It widened then spread into a near circle. My grandfather would not approach it and would not go any further. I kept beckoning him to get closer, but he would not, giving the excuse of a sandbar. "We'll get stuck, he said in French. He then told me how he and his grandfather had gotten stuck by going too close. They had to jump out the boat and push the boat to get it free. He said I was not strong enough to push a stuck boat free of the hold of the suction of that sand formed by the silt.

He told me to settle down, which I did. He then pointed with his finger depicting the exact spot. "Look, do you see it," he asked. I said no.

" 'garde la, droit sous l'eau,", He then said it again, "right underneath the water's surface." he said repeating his first remark. He always spoke in Louisiana Cajun French. I did as he said, and I strained my eyes and then I finally saw it. "It's a post," I said. That's all that is, it's a post". He immediately corrected me and informed me that it was the Mast of what was once a sailing vessel.

"Why was it left there," I questioned. He could not answer, at least, not exactly. He told me that his grandfather had once told him that it was a small boat belonging to Jean Lafitte. He further explained that the men may have vacated the boat to seek escape on land from the law enforcement people. He also said that canon fire may have sunk the boat. Then he added that it could have been that the boat hit a cypress knee in the shallow bayou and took on water. He also said that Jean Laffitte would sometime purposefully sink a boat and leave the treasure on the boat. He said that he usually done so when the law was chasing him.

My young mind was astonished. How do you know this," I asked him. His only response was that such was what his grandfather had told him.

I beckoned him even more to bring me closer. I didn't want to leave. I wanted to figure out a way to get to the boat. His face got real stern as he told me in a rough voice to simmer down.

"Il n' y'a pas rien que tu peut faire," he said explaining that there was nothing that he or I could do. He continued to explain that the boat was buried under a lot of sediment, and it had been there for over a hundred years. This was in the early 1960s.

Jean Lafitte died in or around 1823, according to some sources. To other sources it wasn't until about 1878. Either way the pirate had given up pirating by 1827 and moved on to better things, if he wasn't dead.

Here I was at the boat, looking at the boat's mast. That mast, barely under the water's surface. It was like it was in another world, another time, and as though I could reach that time if I just touched that mast. the image   stayed marked in my mind.

Years later, perhaps 12 years or so after I was grown, I returned with my own boat during a time of very low water. The mast was sticking out the water perhaps a foot or so, at that time. I had brought a metal detector with me. I began scanning the area around the mast. It took quite a few sweeps and it took digging out as much sand as possible away from the area. I also set the machine to its longest reach before I got a beep. It showed an object about the size of a half-dollar.

It informed me that the depth was about 3 feet. I began digging and I would put the mud in the boat to sort through it.

I was about 2 feet under the water. I swept the area again and I began digging to where the detector indicated. But I never could reach it. It stayed out of reach.

I realized that the story my grandfather told me could be, and probably is, true. I was browsing through a collection of microfilm of a newspaper in Napoleonville, a few years later when I spied the announcement of a succession sale. The announcement gave news of the succession of the property of the "Widow of Jean Lafitte". The sale was taking place in Paincourtville, Louisiana. It was just a dozen miles from Pierre Part. It proved that Jean Lafitte did frequent the area. He actually lived in the area and was often in the vicinity of Lake Verret. The boat seemed to be connected to Jean Lafitte. The very boat shown to me by my grandfather had to be a connection to that famous pirate.

The story is absolutely true. Still to this day I want to return, once again and dig for the treasure of Jean Laffitte.

I found out through research that Jean Lafitte had possible relatives living in Labadieville, and also in Thibodaux.

He stayed in Thibodaux quite often when he would take a run with his boat down Bayou Lafourche to out run the law. The law was always in search of him, I have learned.

Yet, he had a relative that was a sheriff in Lafouche Parish. Imagine that, the biggest, most wealthiest pirate of all had friends in law enforcement in South Louisiana not far from Assumption Parish.

There will be those who won't believe a word of it, but I have no reason to lie. Lying would not benefit me whatsoever. The truth is there for the finding, just do the research. Most of the old people who knew of this are now dead. There are families in Labadieville who know of this truth but do not know how to prove it. It is a rath-er difficult thing to prove because of a thing that took place in Acadie. There were things that took place, such as "Le Grand Derangement", that displace people, that ruined records, and during those times records were not always properly kept.

Several churches burnt and along with that went proof and the key to the truth.

What is known for a fact is that Jean Lafitte had property in Paincourtivlle. He had a shop in Paincourtville. There are records of this in local libraries. Remember that Jean Lafitte kept many things secret. He was not a bragger, there are many secret graves with dead men that would attest to this if only they could. Their ghosts allegedly protect buried treasure.

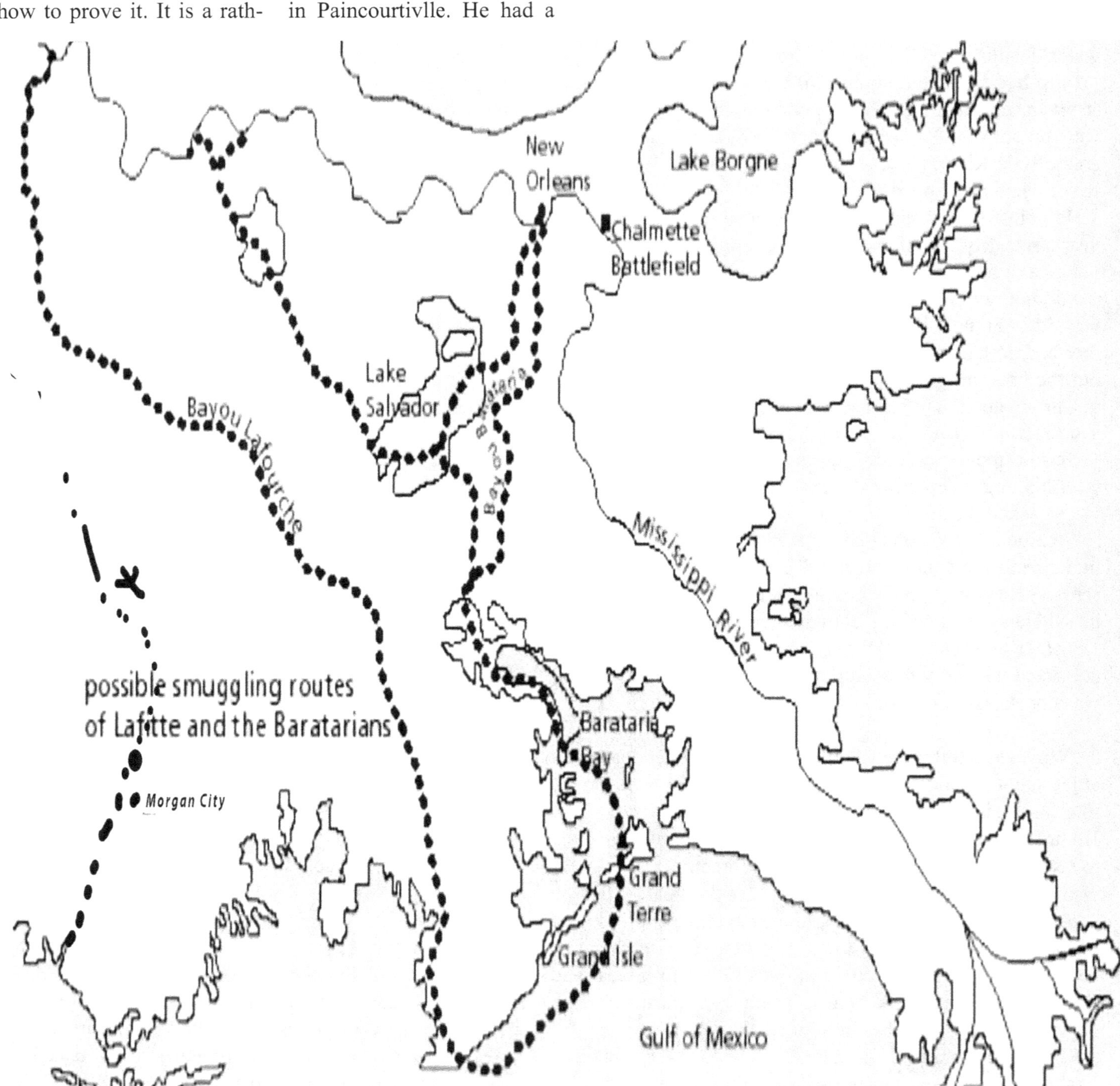

A Brief History of a Pierre Part Mabille family

written by Morgan J. Landry © 2018   Part 1

Emile Joseph Zephyrh Mabille, Sr.

Emile is the son of Arestide Pierre Mabile and the grandson of Jerville Gentil Mabille. Most of his documents list him as Emile Sr.; and he married Emilie Marie Haydel.
 Emile was born on March 10, 1878 in Pierre Part, La. His occupation as a farmer took him to White Castle where he became an overseer on a plantation. Jean Baptiste Mabile, the Civil War soldier whose picture appears in this magazine is Emile's great uncle.

Photo provided by Catherine Mabile Talbot

Emilie Marie "Haydel" Mabille

Marie, [her saint name (middle)] was born in St. John Parish, Louisiana in 1888. She married Emile Joseph Mabille in 1903. Marie and Emile had nine children together. One of their children, whom will be discussed later in the series of articles is Joseph Wilson Mabile who married Clemence E. "Skippy" Berthelot.   Joseph and Clemence settled down in White Castle, La.; and ran a farm in that area. The community is on much higher ground than Pierre Part and contains some very rich farmland.

Photo provided by Catherine Mabile Talbot

In the area of Pierre Part, and other areas where descendants of Mabiles exist, the question sometimes arises as to whom the first Mabile in Louisiana could have been. Due to extensive research that question has been answered.

But first, As you probably noticed in the title of this story, the family name of modern day Mabile is originally spelled as Mabille. For some strange reason the name has created a ton of misspellings and mispronunciations for the English speaking people   through the years. These are more commonly known as "Les anglais." Mabile descendants; and their brothers, sisters and cousins Know about this for quite often les anglais pronounce as mobile.

This story has taken a lot of research and much going back and forth checking facts to make sure the story was accurate. Research on Ancestry took place also, and it is that research that determined that the assumption was true.

Ancestry created a location map of Mabile families and their map shows the first Mabiles in Louisiana around 1880; but that is wrong. 1880 is about the time that the Mabille family had begun to grow in Pierre Part, La. and in White Castle, La.

But Mabiles were here long before ancestry's map shows them as being here. One family of Mabile descendants has provided the necessary proof to validate that claim. In fact, it is quite possible, and yes, most probable, that the large majority of the Mabile descendants, from Louisiana are descended from this one person.

Lisa Daggett , a direct descendant of Emile Joseph Zephyrh Mabile, Sr. and Emilie Marie Haydel Mabile; and her cousin Douglas Mabile of New Orleans provided photos, stories and information that greatly aided in the writing of the story and the successful research on the genealogy of the Mabile family.

Douglas Mabile, a descendant of Gentile Mabile, and Adam Joseph Mabile, provided letters from the early 1800s that carry proof of Gentil Jean Mabile being a resident of Pierre Part , Louisiana during that the early part of the 1800s.

Gentil Jean Mabile, the grandfather of Arestide Pierre Mabile, and the great grandfather of Emile Joseph Zephyrh Mabile, is the first Mabile in Louisiana according to information currently available through modern research.

Documents from the French Consulat show him as being born on June 10, 1810 in La Gironde, France.

La Gironde is one of the original 83 depart-

ments created during the French Revolution on 4 March 1790. It was created from parts of the former provinces of Guyenne and Gascony.

Gentil, whose name means nice, is possibly the first Mabile ever in the United States, also. That for the simple fact that there doesn't seem to be a record of Mabiles in Acadia (Acadie). There is a record of one Mabile in Canada, who died shortly after getting there, in the 1500s.

Extensive research has uncovered that the alleged true name of this Mabile is, for the record, Jerville Gentille Mabile. The name Jean is sometimes thrown in for a middle name on some family trees.

Church records show Gentil Mabile as being married at the age of 28 to Amelina Marie Guillot at the Church of the Assumption in Plattenville, Louisiana on Monday April 16, 1838.

One record from the Catholic Diocese in Baton Rouge lists him as Jerville Gentil Mabile. It lists his birthday and the witnesses. One of the witnesses at the wedding turns out to be Louis Gravereaux, Gentil's good friend from France.

There has also been another discovery, siblings who never traveled here from France.

First of all, Gentil's father is Pierre Mabile born in La Gironde France in 1785,. Gentil's mother is Marie Audry Sutre, born in 1790 in La Gironde, France.

Gentil has three brothers who are Bertrand, Cadiche, and Lonne.

What brought Gentil to Louisiana? How did he get here? Passage aboard a ship was very expensive at that time. That is why some people bonded themselves out to others so as to make the trip; that is how slavery started. But that wasn't the case with Gentil Mabille. He is not found on any passenger list on any ship on record, at least not any that can be found.

What brought Gentil Mabille to Louisiana from France was a love gone wrong, and an argument with his brother Bertrand in France over a girl named Lanon. But, that is only part of the story. There are other factors that contributed to his trip to Louisiana.

His former girlfriend Lanon, no last name given caused him quite a heart ache, according to letters sent to Gentil by his mother. There are several letters, all written in French, but they have been translated to English. There are various other items that belonged to Gentil that Douglas Mabile and Lisa Daggett and the family

want to share with the Mabiles of Pierre Part, La. More information on the Pierre Part, La Facebook page.

First, let's look at comments written by Douglas Mabile, son of Esther and Adam Mabile.

Douglas writes: "It is impossible to know what happened between Gentille Jean Mabile and his parents to cause them to write such powerful letters. Perhaps a serious disagreement caused him to leave his homeland to start a new life in America. Why America? Why Pierre Part?

Some family lore has him as a stowaway on a ship - - other stories -- that he and a brother had a fight over a girl. Perhaps it was simply a business opportunity. It seems from one letter that Gentille and   Louis Gravereaux were from the same town in France.

Mr. Gravereaux was living in Pierre Part and perhaps Gentille was in contact with him. Another bit of lore states that upon his arrival in New Orleans he met someone transporting sugar cane from Bayou Lafourche area (somehow connected with Mr. Gravereaux??) and followed him there. The 1835 letter is addressed to Jean (Gentil)Mabile "Sailor in Louisiana"

The 1850 and 1860 census has Gentil listed as

a farmer."

Douglas also writes that French Scholar he met in New Orleans, specializing in medieval French literature, said that "many people in France from that period did not read or write."

Douglas states , "She (the scholar) was certain that several of the letters were written by a clergyman or perhaps a lawyer. That would explain the dramatic phrasing. For some reason, Gentille, at the age of 24, decided to leave France for a new life in America, thus establishing the Mabiles in Louisiana."

Douglas is correct that Louis Gravereaux and Gentil Mabile were from the same place in France. Louis Gravereaux's birthplace is shown as La Roque, Blai, France. He was born there in 1803. He was about 7 years older than Gentil Mabile. Gentil was born in the same community.

The first letter sent to Louisiana to Gentil Mabile, in care of Louis Gravereaux, was labeled "Fait a La Rogue le 23 Decembre 1835". It simply means, Made at La Rogue. If, indeed, Pierre Mabile or Marie Audry Sutre did not live there they, in fact, went there to get their letters written to Gentil Mabile, in Louisiana.

It is known, as a fact, that Gentil Mabile could

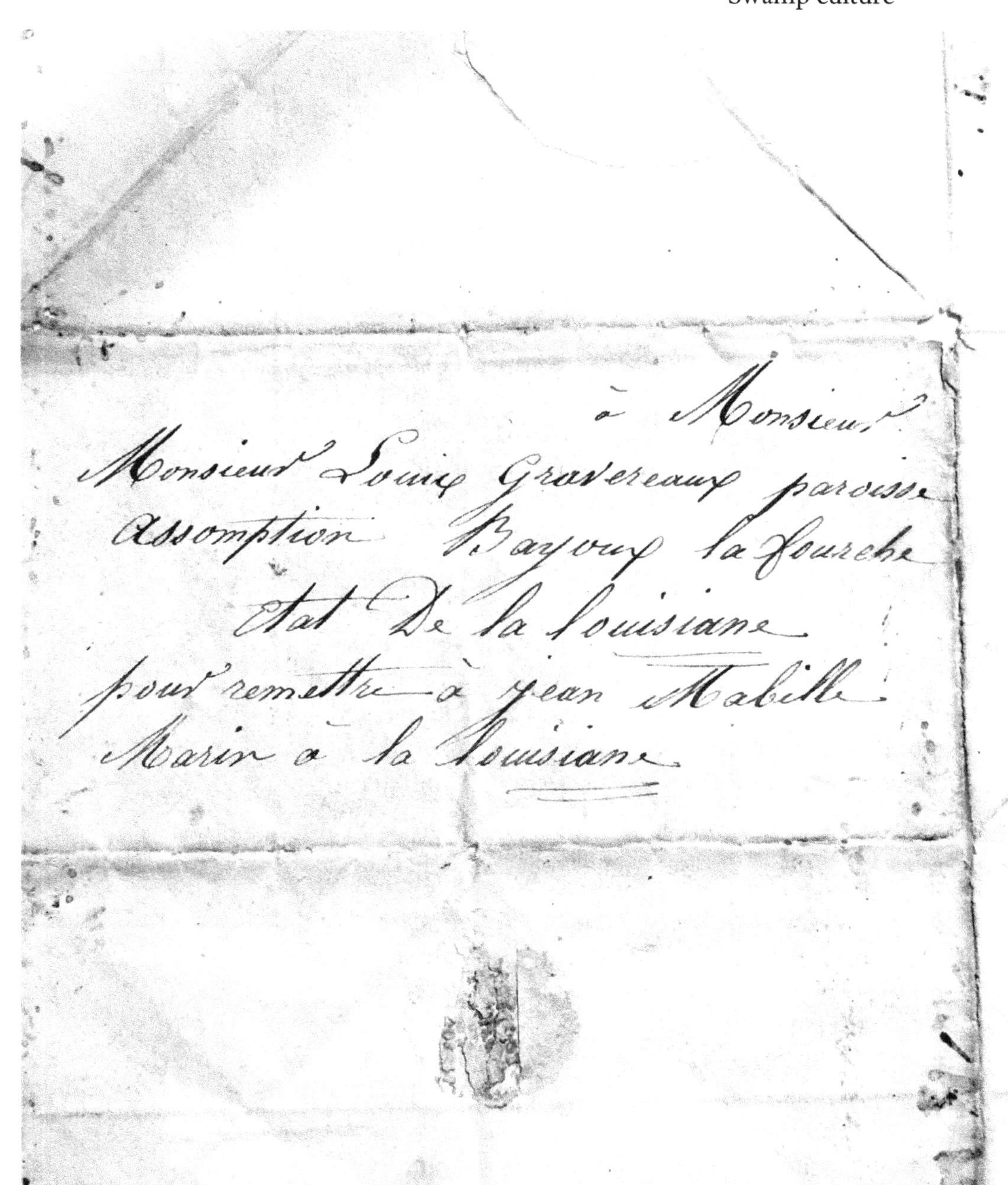

A photo of the actual envelope sent to Gentil Jean Mabile from France. The letter is addressed to Mr. Louis gravereaux, Parish of Assumption, Bayou Lafourche, State of Louisiana.

For remittance to Jean Mabile, Sailor at Louisiana.

Notice that Mabile was spelled with 2 "ls" as Mabille.
That was from the letter sent around 1835.

not read and write. This is documented in the 1830 census. It is also documented in a naturalization document at a much later date in 1865.

As Douglas stated earlier it is very likely that Gentil's parents could not read and write, and would go either to a priest or to a lawyer to get letters written. It was the only way they had of getting it done.

Commoners, more commonly known as peasants to some, were known as the third estate in 18th century France and well into part of the 19th century. This class did not share the privileges of the First and Second Estates. This kept most of the commoners dirt poor and kept them out of schools and anchored to a miserable life. The 1800s brought the age of enlightenment but Gentil left long before that age arrived. He left right at the end of the French revolution and the beginning of Napoleon's short reign of being emperor. That was another reason for leaving France.

As for Gentil I do know that the people of Pierre Part, La. Would stick together. There was always at least one person in the community that could read and write. Most certainly the priest could read and write if no one else could. I can

remember the days of my youth in Pierre Part where people would go to people who had schooling to get letters written or read. I saw that happen often during that time. The number of people who could not sign their name was totally astounding. It's funny how the lack of education, because of the dark ages sort of trickled into the 20th century. Over a hundred years before illiteracy stopped being a majority thing in this area of Pierre Part and its sister community of Belle River.

Douglas Mabile is correct in his synopsis that Gentil Mabile and Louis Gravereaux were from the same town in France.

Louis Gravereaux was born in 1803 in the same general area Gentil Mabile was born in 1810. Both were born in La Gironde in France. That area, La Gironde is one of the original 83 departments created during the French Revolution on 4 March 1790. It was created from parts of the former provinces of Guyenne and Gascony.

That leads to another thing that causes people to leave their country of origin. We are seeing refugees from many countries these days, some wanting to flood the United States because they are not happy with their country of

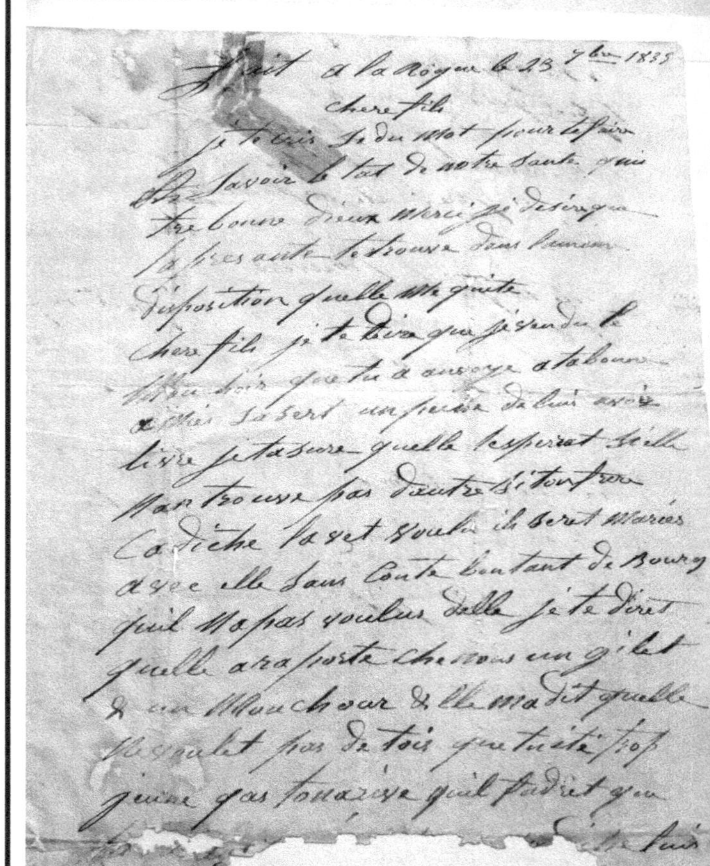

Une lettre de ses parents

A photo of the actual   1835 letter sent to Gentil Mabile

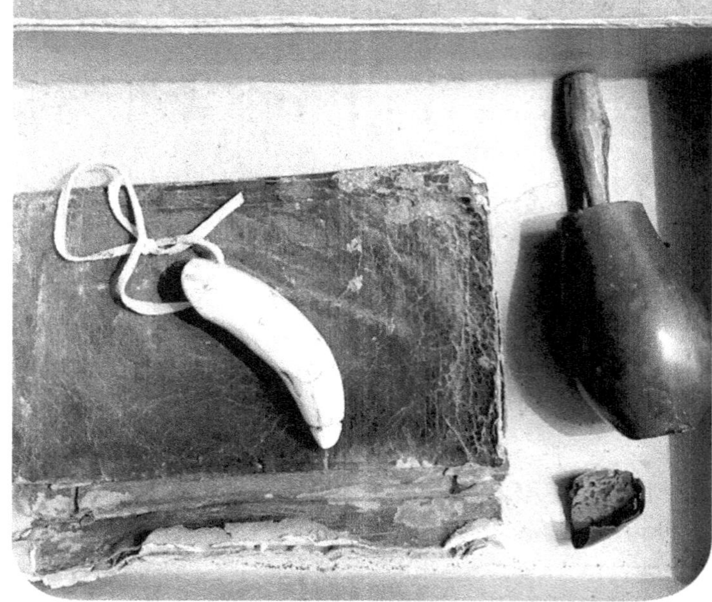

Gentil Mabile's Powder Horn

The black-powder horn is fabricated from the tusk of a wild boar. Directly under the horn is a type of leather satchel or pouch that Gentil mabile used to carry his letters and such.

origin.

At the time that Louis Gravereaux and Gentil were born they were coming into the world at the end of the reign of terror caused by the French revolution.

Napoleon was in the process of becoming the first emperor of France. That was not a happy time.

There were many battles being fought, against Britain, for it was the only one remaining to face Napoleon.

The battle of waterloo took place just 5-years after Gentil was born. It was a very rough time in France. It was not a very good place to be at that time.

Douglas Mabile Stated earlier, in his comments, that Gentile came to the United States at the age of 24. That is correct as far as can be determined. It is the best possible assumption that can be made because of the little documentation available. However,

United States of America,

DEPARTMENT OF THE GULF.

Nº

Office Provost Marshal General.

New Orleans, ss. I, *Gentille Mabile* do solemnly swear that I am a subject of *France* that I have never become or been a Citizen of the **United States,** by naturalization or otherwise, nor have I declared my intention to become such Citizen. That I have never held any political office, nor voted at any political election in the **United States,** nor done any act in derogation of my allegiance to *the French Government*

I DO FURTHER SOLEMNLY SWEAR, that so long as my Government remains at peace with the **United States** I will do no act, nor aid, advise or consent that any be done, nor conceal any act done or to be done, that shall aid, assist or comfort any of the enemies or opposers of the **United States,** or the authority or Government thereof.

Sworn before me this 25th

day of *May* 186 5

Gentile his X *Mabile* mark

The document that Gentil Mabile had to sign when the Provost Marshal General found him in Pierre Part. Gentil had entered the country illegally, never became naturalized and had to put his mark on this paper to start the process to become naturalized. Gentil Mabile became a citzen of the United States in 1870.

new documentation has been discovered. It still does not reveal the year he came here but it does reveal how he may have arrived.

NOTATION FOUND ON ANCESTRY: "Note: Gentel Mabile (FG 52)

Informed sources say, Gentel Mabile came to Louisiana from France by boat, along with many courageous travelers. Some disembarked at Thibadeaux, Pierre Part and Donaldsonville, which the latter is where Gentel Mabile decided to remain after once before disembarking with a friend at Thibadeaux. There is in existence a letter written by his mother Marie Sudre Mabile, asking him to return to France. This original letter is in the possession of Adam Mabile of Napoleonville, La. "

It is now known that Louis Gravereaux and Gentil Mabile traveled together to Louisiana. It was first thought that Louis came to Louisiana first and then invited his friend over to Louisiana. The note now confirms that they traveled together with others. This now confirms that Gentil Mabile was not a stowaway. It is known that he was not yet a citizen of the United States when he became married to a local girl by the name of Amelina Marie Guillot in 1838.

However, it also reveals, more than likely, the final reason as to why Gentil, his friend Louis, and the boatload of companions came to Louisiana. The sugar industry was starting to come alive in Louisiana!

An article titled "The Modernization of the Louisiana Sugar Industry, 1830-1910" written by John Alfred Heitmann (1987) states that : "During the 1820s word spread that great prof-

its could be made from planting sugarcane. The dream of riches lured both footloose fortune hunters and entire families from New England, New York, Virginia, North Carolina, Ireland, and elsewhere to this lush, semitropical, and in many ways mysterious, region." In the 1830s technology improved for creating a better sugar and the word of making money spread again.

Gentil was just turning

20 years old in 1830. It is entirely possible that he came to Louisiana between 1830 and 1834. Maybe even when he was 18. That part will remain a mystery unless paper work on the ship is located, a ship log or a passenger log.

Life in Pierre Part came to a head in 1865 for the Mabiles. Life came to an end for Amelina Marie Guillot Mabile, wife of Gentil Mabile on the first of May 1865. Cause of

Arestide Pierre Mabile born September 7, 1849 is the son of Jerville Gentille Mabile and Amelina Marie Guillot. He is part of the first generation of Mabiles born on American soil, born on Louisiana soil, a true creole as defined in Louisiana Cajun French. He is not Acadian. Gentil Mabile, his father came here directly from France. His mother, Amelina Marie Guillot - her grandfather came here directly from France. Fabian Amateur Guillot Sr. was born in Trigavou, Cotes de Nord in France.

Photo provided by Douglas Mabile

death is unknown but it is known that the Civil war was still being fought in some places. The Rebel armies were eager for more manpower, the Union Armies were in the area, etc. Of course, yellow fever was always a threat in the area. Death was forever present in the swamp waiting to take another victim.

The Civil War ended on April 9, 1865. During those days it took very long for news to travel, sometimes months. It is said that it took close to a year and a half for news of the Civil War ending to reach everyone. That could be some of the reason as to why Amelina Marie Guillot Mabile died on May 1, 1865. Was she trying to protect her husband from Union Soldiers? She was only 45-years old.

Could soldiers or the Marshal have been there on the first of May? Thus far it remains a secret. The search will continue and any new information on Gentil or his spouse Amelina will be revealed in the next story in Part II of the Mabile Family History.

It is known that the Provost Marshal was there to serve papers to Gentille Mabile on May 25, 1865. The reason that is known is that the paper which Gentil signed is in the possession of Douglas Mabile of New Orleans.

It is known that the Marshal and possibly soldiers were at Gentil's home in Pierre Part in the month of May in 1865.

The 1860 Census showed Gentil and his wife and family in Pierre Part. Gentil was listed as a farmer. The census takers, most of whom had very little education and some who could not read French spelled Mabille as Mobile. Gentil was listed as being 55 years of age in this census.

Joseph Clairville was listed as being 21, Jean Baptiste was listed as being 18, Mannette was listed as 13, Pierre as 12, Louisa as 9 and Elisabeth as 5.

In the 1970 census a couple of surprises are there. There is the presence of another child. A child by the name of Adressaie is present and she is listed as being five years of age. It is quite possible, very probable that Amelina Marie Guillot Mabille died of child birth on May 1, 1865. After all , the baby was born in May and the mother died on May 1st.

In this same census the family name is spelled as Mabille , once again.

Clairville is listed by his first name now. The problem with some genealogy databases, especially those listed by the Catholic Diocese is that the Saint name of the person (middle name) is listed first. That is why some people think it is the person's first name.

The children of Gentil Jean Mabile and Amelina Marie Guillot Mabile are: Arestide Pierre Mabille; Annette Mabille; Amelia Mabille; Jean Baptiste Mabille; Clairville Joseph Mabille; Elisabeth Mabille; Louise Mabille; Adresaie Mabille; and Mariette Mabille.

All the children were at their father's home in Pierre Part when his death drew near. Gentil allegedly died in 1870 but an exact date of his death can not be located.

The Catholic Diocese in Baton Rouge communicated by email that there are missing records, that they have gaps in their records. They have records on Gentil's wife, Amelina Marie Guillot, but do not yet have the records on Gentil Mabile.

LETTERS --

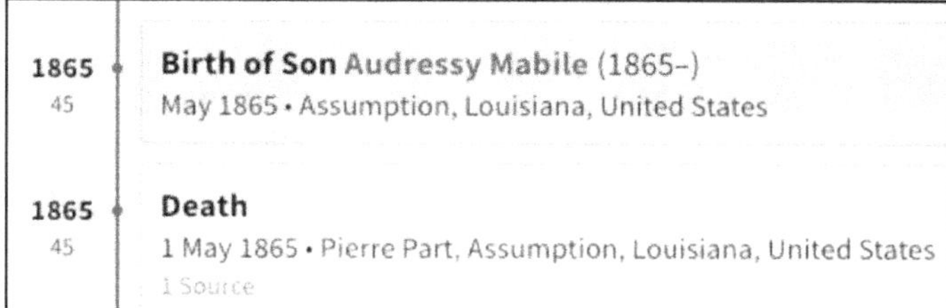

bases, especially those listed by the Catholic Diocese is that the Saint name of the person (middle name) is listed first. That is why some people think it is the person's first name.

Even though Marie Audry Sudre (mother of Gentil Mabile) had three other sons in France of whom she could request assistance it seems that every letter she sent carried a request for money from Gentil.

She would throw in little petty insults, what the Cajuns call "des fions". The word fion has changed in modern French but in old French, such as the one used in Pierre Part it means an insult.

No one really know the reason why she always bugged Gentil but it could be something as Doug stated.

It seemed, as it had once been stated by Doug Mabile, that she thought that Gentil was making a fortune in Louisiana.

Gentil would often reply with a

snide remark. This is known due the fact of the responses from his mother. There was this one time she asked for money that he responded with: "J'avait sauve 300 francs mais j l'ai user pour mon plaisir." That translates to : I had saved 300 francs but I used it for my own pleasure. To me that is what is called "un fion". Languages change over time. The modern definition is not the exact same as the old-age defini-tion. It also varies by region. According to Emile Littre's Dic-tionaire de la langue française the Etymol-ogie (history) of the word Fion is of Suisse origin and the original meaning is un mot pi-quant, moquerie. That means a spicy mock-ing t word. And that is exactly what Gentil Mabille was doing to his mother. He was mocking her, throwing in some words that would burn like fire. The Louisiana French, like the French rela-tives in Acadia and France have a special term for it that I can not write or convey here. It's much too spicy. That's how the old French culture is and it remains how it was until the 1970s

here in Louisiana, especially in Pierre Part. The only ones who remember it are the old timers, the native speakers which remain. Many of the younger people have lost that touch, that ability to spice up the language. They never paid enough attention or their parents did not want to teach them. They were afraid that their children would suffer the same misery as they did.

The Mabile Family Crest

The section of the 1870 United States Federal Census for Amelie Mabille

Louisiana > Assumption > Ward 13

Name	Age	Sex	Race	Occupation	Real Estate	Personal Estate	Birthplace	Fath Forei	Moth Forei	Birth Month	Marria Month	Attended	Cannot R	Cannot W	Condition	Male Ove	Denied Voting
Girir Clare	26	M	W	Farmer		150	Louisiana								1 1		1
" Virginie	22	F	W	Keeping house			Louisiana								1 1		
" Idea	7	F	W				Louisiana										
" Alisina	4	F	W				Louisiana										
" Henry	1	M	W				Louisiana										
Mabille Gentile	60	M	W	Farmer	450	300	France	1	1						1 1		1
" Clairville	30	M	W				Louisiana								1 1		1
" Jean B.te	28	M	W				Louisiana	1							1 1		1
" Amelie	26	F	W				Louisiana	1							1 1		
" Mariette	24	F	W				Louisiana	1							1 1		
" Louise	21	F	W				Louisiana	1							1 1		
" Aristide	20	M	W				Louisiana	1							1 1		
" Elisabeth	17	F	W				Louisiana	1							1 1		
" Madelaine	8	F	W				Louisiana	1									
" Adrienne	5	M	W				Louisiana	1									
Girir Aristide	23	M	W	Farmer	200	300	Louisiana								1 1		1

No. of dwellings, _______ No. of white females, _______ No. of males, foreign born, _______ No. of insane, _______

" " families, _______ " " colored males, _______ " females, _______ " blind, _______

" " white males, _______ " females, _______ " blind, _______

7 of 16

The section of the 1870 Census depicting Gentile Mabile and family minus Amelina Marie Guillot Mabille. Either the children were still living with him at the time of the census or they were at the house at the time of the census, possibly taking care of their father. He allegedly died during that year.

South Louisiana New Year's Traditions

story by Morgan J. Landry

Jour de L'an chez ma ma

J'ai rêver hier soir que ç'était jour de l'an et que j'été visiter mémére. That translates to: "I dreamed last night it was New Year's day and I went visit my MaMa.

New Year's day was so wonderful back then, in fact, more than wonderful. The first place I would go to was to Gram Corrine. Then to Memére Françoise, Then, at one point in the early morning, my pépére Claiborne would take me visiting all throughout the neighborhood. Such wonderful memories of those years. Also funny is how my tastebuds also have memories of those special days which comprised the first 10 years or so of my life. Those wonderful Cajun traditions of visiting people on New Year's day, I wish they would never have ended.

In those times, which were the mid-1950s thru the mid-1960s visiting neighbors was a very common practice of the time. Facebook did not exist, not too many people enjoye TV because it was all English an they only spoke French. But they did enjoy, immensely those programs in Cajun French such as the Lafayette Playboys on Channel 10 in Lafayette.

So, where did this tradition come from? Was it a practice of just the Cajuns or how did it get started?

Well according to research the practice was carried with our ancestors from France. It was carried to la nouvelle france, which was l'acadie (now Nova Scotia); and then carried over to Louisiana. Also, many of the people who cam here directly from France, such as Gentille Mabile and others of other families brought their traditions with them.

Information was found on the French vesion of Wikipedia. The search term used was Jour de l'an. New Year's Day in English. One example is: "Belgique --

En Belgique, il est de tradition de faire la tournée de ses amis et familles afin de leur souhaiter la bonne année. Ceux-ci offrent en général, un verre d'alcool (goutte) ainsi qu'une assiette de galettes.

Les enfants prononcent des vœux (en poème ou non) devant leurs grands parents ou parents et en guise de remerciement, reçoivent une "dringuelle" (du flamand "drink geld") c'est-à-dire

des étrennes." The translation is a follows: "Belgium

In Belgium, it is traditional to tour friends and families to wish them a Happy New Year. These usually offer a glass of alcohol (drop) and a plate of patties.

Children make wishes (poem or not) in front of their grandparents or parents and as a thank you, receive a "dringual" (Flemish "drink geld") that is to say new year gifts.

Now, one more example is one from France: "France

Baiser sous le gui, huile sur toile de Karl Witkowski (ici dépeignant la même tradition aux États-Unis).

Le jour est férié en France.

En Savoie, au Jour de l'an et au mois de janvier, on donnait des cornets de friandises ou de l'argent aux enfants, appelés étrennes, à chaque fois que l'on rendait visite à des membres de la famille. Le Jour de l'an, on rendait visite à des amis pour souhaiter la bonne année.

C'est à ce moment de l'année que le personnel de maison, les gardiens, concierges, etc., reçoivent leurs étrennes, une somme d'argent versée par l'employeur qui récompense ainsi la qualité du service rendu au cours de l'année écoulée.

À minuit, une tradition veut que les Français se fassent la bise sous une branche de gui.

On peut présenter ses vœux jusqu'au 31 janvier12.

Translated this comes out to: "

Kiss under the mistletoe, oil on canvas by Karl Witkowski, referrring to a painting, (here depicting the same tradition in the United States).

The day is a holiday in France.

In Savoy, on New Year's Day and in January, children were given candy rings or money, called new presents, whenever family members were visited. New Year's Day, we visited friends to wish the good year.

It is at this time of the year that the house staff, the caretakers, caretakers, etc., receive their gifts, a sum of money paid by the employer which thus rewards the quality of the service rendered during the year. past year.

At midnight, a tradition wants the French to kiss under a branch of mistletoe.

His wishes may be presented until 31 January12.

In Acadie and parts of Canada the tradition is/or was as follows: "Canada

Au Canada français et en Acadie, le Nouvel An est un évènement qui se fête en famille. Ainsi, comme dans le « bon vieux temps », les membres des parentés se rassemblent dans de vieilles maisons familiales lors de veillées festives. Chez plusieurs Canadiens français et Acadiens, le temps du Jour de l'an est donc une période particulièrement riche en vieilles traditions. Un hommage spécial est alors rendu à la musique traditionnelle dont les origines remontent à l'époque de la colonie : chanson à répondre, cotillon, gigue, podorythmie, quadrille (set carré), reel, rigodon, etc. Dindes, pâtés de viande, ragoût de pattes de cochon, atocas, betteraves, gâteaux aux fruits, sont parmi les aliments qui composent traditionnellement le menu du repas du Jour de l'an. Mais, avant de commencer la fête et sur demande de l'aîné des enfants, plusieurs familles procèdent d'abord à la bénédiction paternelle.

Plusieurs personnes préfèrent cependant fêter le passage au nouvel an dans un bar. De plus, au Québec, le Bye Bye est une émission de télévision qui fait une revue humoristique de l'année qui s'achève. Elle est diffusée de 1968 à 1998 et par la suite, depuis 2006. Cette émission est présentée le

31 décembre à 23 h sur les ondes de Radio-Canada, une tradition pour plusieurs Québécois."

Translation: Canada

In French Canada and Acadia, the New Year is an event that is celebrated with the family. Thus, as in the "good old days", family members gather in old family houses during festive evenings. For many French and Acadian Canadians, New Year's Day is a particularly rich period in old traditions. A special tribute is then paid to the traditional music whose origins go back to the time of the colony: song to answer, cotillon, jig, podorythmie, quadrille (square set), real, rigodon, etc. Turkeys, meat pies, pork leg stew, cranberries, beets, fruit cakes, are among the foods that traditionally make up the New Year's Day meal menu. But before the party begins and at the request of the eldest child, several families first proceed to the paternal blessing.

Many people, however, prefer to celebrate New Year's Eve at a bar. In addition, in Quebec Bye Bye is a television show that makes a humorous review of the year that is coming to an end. It was broadcast from 1968 to 1998 and subsequently since 2006. The show is being shown on December 31 at 11 pm on Radio-Canada, a tradi-

tion for many Quebeckers.

That last one sounds more like what we have expereienced in Louisiana during the latter part of the 1950s and early 1960s. The traditions have faded away there as well. From what I remember of those days, and knowing my relatives as they were at one time, the celebrating at a bar sounds a lot more like Pierre Part and Belle River used to be back in the day from what it is today.

There are several friends who have shared their memories with us.

Lois Viguet, formerly a Daigle, shared some memories. She wrote: "

Morgan Landry do you remember a tradition as young children we would go from neighbor to neighbor on New Year's Day and wish them Bon Jour and Bon ane! And I probably didn't pronounce it correctly! Julie and I talked about experiencing that as kids' it was our tradition on Belle River to do that for years. Our neighbors had the best Popcorn balls, fudge, candy and what ever they had to share!"

Yes, such wonderful memories during those times I certainly wish I could help in returning them to the present.

I responded to Lois' comment with: "Lois Viguet - I certainly do remember, yes indeed. My grandfather would bring me around the neighborhood. I remember we would go to Taunte Claire and my grandfather had a saying he would say: bonjour a la bonne année, je vous souhaite une bonne année et une bonne santée pour la balance de tes jours.

Taunte Claire would make some delicious tarte a la bouille every year for New Year's Day, There was this one time I went I asked for seconds and thirds. We would go to everyone in the neighborhood, Lois Viguet, Just like you and Julie Troxclaire would do, and we'd come back with a bunch of delicious popcorn balls. I always ate the Tartes a la bouillee on site. Ms. Claire would somehow manage to pack a few slices for us to bring home. Those popcorn balls were coated with delicious sugar cane syrup. My grandmother and my mom would make cakes way ahead of the holiday. My grandmother also would make some tartes a la bouille and what a treat that was so much of that delicious custard pie at home.

What a wonderful day New Years Day was way back then when we were kids. Wish I could go back and visit because the most wonderful thing about it is that everyone spoke French. The second most wonderful thing is that

parents and grandparents spent time with their children and grandchildren.

Julie Troxclaire responded with: Awesome, Those were the most loving times, people had their doors and hearts open. Great memories, that's when we knew everybody in Belle River.

Casey Sedotal, formerly a Breaux, said that, "I remember doing this as a child. Later my dad would go visit all his kids and give all the grandkids a couple of 50-cent pieces.

Evelyn Simoneaux said that: "I remember it like it was yesterday. We would go to church and on the way home we would stop at Mamere Theriot's house, and she would give us popcorn balls made from the cane syrup Papere Theriot would make in the syrup mill in the back. Of course, everyone was greeted with 'Bonne Année'. Those were wonderful days."

The tradition was similar for everyone in the Pierre Part community, even in Belle River; but everyone had their own little thing they did and they did it their way. That was the beauty of it, and the most important part of it is that it was all family oriented. Children were very respectful back then, we dared not disrespect an elder. It's nothing like today's world.

Rodney Perera said that, "My dad would open

the grocery store half a day on New Years Day and greet customers with BONJOUR LA BON ANNEE...!!"

I responded with -- Rodney I used to love going to your Dad's store. It was one of the best in the area and he had such a wonderful personality. Great gentleman he was. I was sad when I heard of his passing.

My great grandfather, Pépére Gustin would make toys for his great grandchildren. These toys were found under the Christmas tree on New Year's day. He would come over to the house and he would say: "Je vois que la Christine t'ramener des toupie," he would say. The first time I remember him making some he took one in his hand and showed me how he had carved the wooden thread spool towards a point, then through the center, where the factory had punched a hole he inserted a match and placed a point on one end so it would have a spinning point. The remainder of the match, more than likely a kitchen match, stuck out of the top and left enough to grab it with the thumb and forefinger and give it a good spin. It was fun and I enjoyed playing with them. That top he made for me, I wished I would have saved one, but more than likely it was a tradition carried over from

the 1800s. He was born in 1882, and I was always fascinated with that because it was knowledge across centuries. He was old enough to have shook hands with Billy the Kid or Wyatt Earp. As I grew older the more I appreciated knowing him.

Gramme Francoise, sometimes I called her mémére, she always had some wonderful cookies and other treats. She called her contributions "des 'tits cadeau" which translates to small gifts. It was such a wonderful time of year for family, and more so than it is in today's world. In the year 2019 children come to visit and most are stuck on their cell phones either playing games or texting. It wasn't like that back then, times were much more enjoyable back then with the families.

Family time was a time of gathering together and listening to each other's conversations. Visting, the women would talk to the women and the men to the men. When the women would get too noisy they would go outside where they could hear each other.

The women would talk about household stuff and get tips from each other. Wonderful, wholesome times they were then.

About the Author

Morgan J. Landry is a native of Pierre Part, Louisiana. He is a journalist, writer, photographer, poet, historian, editor, reporter,author, and researcher.

He is also a husband, father, grandfather, and Christian.

He began his journalism career at Nicholls State University in Thibodaux, La. He earned his Bachelor's degree in journalism at Ashford University in Iowa. He also earned a Master of Arts in Education from Ashford University.

He has written for 8 newspapers in Louisiana of which he was the Editor-n-chief of The Eagle Tribune News in Pierre Part. Some of his articles are on file at the Ashford University Library.

His scholarly articles such as -- "The Navajo Indian in America The destruction of a Nation by the European Caucasians in the United States" is searched on a daily basis.

His Christian poetry draws some attention also because of its deep felt, heart warming lines crying out to the King of Kings.

His novelette on poetry - "Poems of Praise to my Savior and King" is being released in May of 2019.

Louisiana Swamp Culture 2 is due for re-release this year, also. In it are included a feature story on Chem-trails and also a feature story on Rhythm and Blues singer Van Broussard.

His biggest project, still in the works, is a book on memories of life in Pierre Part, La.

Titled "Stories of Ol' Pierre Part" the book features a brief history of the small Cajun town and the way of life in the swamps and on the bayous of Louisiana during that period long ago.

In his writings Morgan Landry conveys the deep roots of the Acadian Culture in Louisiana, he even drives home the importance of being Louisiana Cajun French in this community; and its Acadian heritage.

The love of being a true Acadien descendant has never left him, he envisions himself first as a servant of God, then a grandfather, husband, a provider, and always reminds family and those willing to listen of the importance of being a child of God first and then "who we are" as being equally important.

.The reason as to why who we are is so important is because without culture we are nothing. We are actually lost without culture.

Morgan uses the quote, "Each individual is born with a personal variant of an inherited genetic template, known as the genome, which has evolved during the entire life span of the human species". It is who we are, thereby we have an essential need to know our history,

Morgan J. Landry
Journalist/writer

our ancestors, our heritage, our culture to know where we have been, what we have done, so that we can correct the future and live better lives.

He believes, as anthropology teaches, that we are all interconnected, interrelated, and come from the same maker. Thereby, we can , and should, push our differences to the side and all live together and love our neighbors and help our neighbors. That is what we are brought into this world with because children do not have any animosity towards each other. Children show more love than adults often do. Thereby Morgan believes that saving our Louisiana Swamp Culture is essential because people in the swamp help each other and love each other as fellow human beings. "Allons préserve notre culture."

Let's save our culture.